*The Psychology
of Religion*

HISTORICAL
AND
INTERPRETATIVE
READINGS

The Psychology of Religion

HISTORICAL AND INTERPRETATIVE READINGS

Edited by ORLO STRUNK, Jr.

ABINGDON PRESS   Nashville and New York

TO MY STUDENTS

Preface

Over a decade has passed since the publication of *Readings in the Psychology of Religion*. In the Preface to that volume I observed that there were "some strong indications of a resurgent interest in the psychology of religion," an observation, I venture to claim, which since has been verified in several important respects.

The publication of at least a dozen exciting new texts and general books in the field, all mentioned in the latter chapters of this book, indicates a continual interest in the psychological study of religion. The resurrection following World War II of the International Association for Psychology of Religion and its journal, *Archiv für Religionspsychologie,* marks even an international awakening to the field, as did the establishment in 1966 of the Quinquennial Prize in the Psychology of Religion. And, of course, the obvious success of the Society for the Scientific Study of Religion and its medium, the *Journal for the Scientific Study of Religion,* partly at least may be seen as a sign of a determination to continue the field known as the psychology of religion. Even more recently plans for the resurrection of G. Stanley Hall's old publication, *Journal of Religious Psychology,* point to a renewed interest in the field.

When one considers the many quiet pressures to "transform" or homogenize the psychology of religion with such popular fields as pastoral care and counseling or pastoral theology, it is quite amazing that the psychology of religion has been able to maintain any identity at all. Although the theological schools frequently have tended to squeeze the discipline out of the curriculum under the canopy of the Practical, when it has lost ground there it has taken on even greater recognition in other settings. As I write this Preface, for instance, I note that one of the sections of the 1970 meeting of the International Association for the History of Religions is devoted to the psychology of religion. That Religious Studies may come to embrace the psychology of religion is a substantial possibility.

It seems to me that in all these developments there is still need to achieve a certain historical perspective, especially in times when students of a field of inquiry do not always appreciate or even acknowledge the past accomplishments of those workers who have gone before them. Presently, the following essays are the closest thing we have to a genuine history of the psychology of religion. As in *Readings in the Psychology of Religion,* I trust that these chapters will provide students with something of a history and interpretation of the field. Clergymen, religious educators, psychologists and psychiatrists, seminarians, and that new breed of students of Religious Studies might well find the following chapters a good first look at a fascinating field of inquiry. At least that is the major purpose of this revision and extension of what originally was the first section of *Readings in the Psychology of Religion.*

As I noted in the *Readings,* a collection such as this represents the contributions of numerous persons besides the editor. Obviously, the many copyright holders are greatly responsible for such a volume. Without their permission to reprint material the book could not have come into existence.

Besides those individuals gratefully acknowledged in the first edition of this book, I should like to mention several other persons who assisted me in preparing this revision. I am especially grateful to Fr. Kevin Culligan, O.C.D., my faculty assistant during the 1969-70 school year, for checking the many references found at the end of this book.

As might be expected, a great deal of time and effort were spent in providing the reader with what I hope will prove to be a sound and functional index, so essential in a book with historical and reference propensities. In this regard, I once again publicly thank my wife, Mary Louise, for her invaluable assistance.

Finally, I wish to express my appreciation to my former students at West Virginia Wesleyan College, and my more recent students at Boston University School of Theology, for taking the time to find out what the psychology of religion is all about and for expressing their own views with clarity and feeling.

O. S.

SCITUATE, MASSACHUSETTS
AUGUST 1, 1970

Contents

Contents

The Psychology of Religion

James Bissett Pratt

A S EVERYONE KNOWS, PSYCHOLOGY IS A WORD TO CONJURE WITH. WE HAVE today the Psychology of Art, the Psychology of Business, the Psychology of Advertising, the Psychology of Childhood, of Adolescence, and of Old Age, the Psychology of various great men and of various centuries and epochs, until one stands quite aghast at the psychological insight of our times, and feels that the key to everything and anything worth knowing must surely be in the hands of the omniscient psychologist. In fact, psychology would seem to have enlarged her bounds at the expense of every other subject, and to have chosen all knowledge to be her province; so that he who desires his book or treatise on any subject whatever to be regarded as strictly "modern" and "scientific" must needs endow it with a psychological title. This is indeed a short and easy method of becoming a psychologist; and the result is—as one might expect—that all the psychology contained in many of these works is spread, usually in large letters, upon the title-page. All is not gold that glitters; neither is every treatise psychological which bears that mystic word upon its cover.

In no field of serious inquiry are these remarks more pertinent than in that of religion. Our book-shelves and our periodicals are laden with works on "religious psychology," most of which prove on examination to be hardly more psychological than anatomical or geographical. Treatises on theology and statistics, on Church history and Sunday-school methods, as well as that large and amorphous class of writings which twenty years ago would have appeared under the title "Philosophy of Religion"—all these are now pressing themselves upon our attention by the use of that potent shibboleth, "Psychology." And yet, though one-half the works with titles of this nature have not much more to do with genuine psychology than with the weather, there is, I believe, a young branch of scientific inquiry which rightly deserves the name Psychology of Religion.

Reprinted by permission of the publishers from *Harvard Theological Review* #1. Cambridge, Mass.: Harvard University Press, 1908.

The attempt to treat the religious consciousness psychologically did not come altogether out of the blue: like other branches of science, it had its precursors of various sorts. The most important of these were anthropology and the history of religion, on the one hand, and the philosophy of religion, on the other. Since the days of Kant it had been customary for writers on the latter subject to take up incidentally the question of the psychological nature of religion, especially in their attempts at defining their subject-matter. These discussions brought out a good many psychological distinctions and descriptions of more or less value; but no attempt was made to collect data and study them inductively in modern scientific fashion. This lack of an empirical basis makes it impossible to accept the results of the various philosophies of religion as genuine psychology; though as the expressions of religious men, and therefore as data bearing on the religious consciousness, they are often of considerable indirect value. The work of the anthropologists, on the other hand, though thoroughly empirical, is from the objective or external point of view, and therefore, while furnishing valuable material to the psychologist, is not itself psychology.

The psychology of religion is therefore, as I have said, a very young branch of inquiry, being in fact hardly more than a dozen years old. I shall not attempt to say who started it. Perhaps no one can justly claim that honor; but, if it can be given to any one man, it must be awarded to President G. Stanley Hall, of Clark University. This I say both because of his own pioneer work in this field and still more because of his guiding influence over a number of young psychologists doing graduate work under him on subjects chosen at his suggestion. Thus was formed what one may very properly call the Clark school of religious psychology.

The work seems to have taken its start in some investigations concerning the various phenomena of adolescence. In 1882 Dr. Hall published an article in the *Princeton Review* entitled "The Moral and Religious Training of Children," in which he emphasized the importance of the years between twelve and sixteen, the sudden changes in both mind and body and the new birth of energy and feeling that take place during that period. This subject was taken up again a number of years later by two graduate students of Clark University, Mr. William H. Burnham (1891)[1] and Mr. Arthur H. Daniels (1895) whose investigations, based upon empirical data gathered in part from responses to questionnaires, in part from the facts of anthropology, lie well within the field of the psychology of religion.[2]

The investigations thus far referred to, though valuable, owe their chief

[1] Bibliographical references will be identified by inserting the publication date after the author's name. The complete reference is given in the bibliography at the end of the volume.
[2] If space permitted, mention should be made of the investigations in the religion of childhood by Hall, Barnes, Brown, and others, carried on at this same time.

importance to their pioneer character. It was not until the year 1896 that the first article of great intrinsic value appeared; namely, the first of a long series of important papers by Mr. James H. Leuba (1896) (also, at that time, of Clark University), entitled "The Psychology of Religious Phenomena." The subject of the work, as was natural for a pioneer attempt, was that most striking of religious phenomena, conversion. Mr. Leuba went at his task in thoroughly scientific fashion. He collected materials for his study from various sources, especially from the published accounts of the conversions of distinguished leaders, and also by means of a questionnaire. Basing his conclusions on these empirical data, he analyzed the psychological conditions leading up to conversion, the crisis itself, and the state following it; he described the mental condition of the enthusiastic believer (the "faith state"), showed the necessity of self-surrender as a precondition of conversion, and the sudden and passive nature of the transition when it finally came; and thus displayed the psychological basis for the Christian doctrines of faith, justification, pardon, etc. The whole process was treated from the naturalistic point of view, the causal sequences traced, and the idea of supernatural intervention ruled out. "We must conceive of faith," says Leuba, "as supervening upon specific and always identical psychological phenomena."

This naturalistic attitude dominates in a general way all the writers in this field, but no others have carried it through so consistently and emphasized it so strongly and, I may add, so dogmatically, as has Leuba. It is the keynote of nearly all the papers from his pen which have appeared in rather quick succession since 1896. These contributions of his are of varying degrees of excellence; they often repeat each other, and at times attempt too great simplification; yet in their consistent scientific point of view and their keen psychological analysis they form a body of writings of very great value and importance. Professor Leuba is a genuine and able psychologist, and his contributions have a right to the name "psychology of religion." They deserve a much wider reading than they have yet enjoyed.[3]

The year after Leuba's first article appeared, two other graduate students of Clark University, under the influence and guidance of Dr. Hall, entered the field, Mr. Edwin D. Starbuck (1903) and Mr. E. G. Lancaster (1895). The interest of the latter was chiefly in the adolescent period as such, while the work of the former was wholly upon the religious questions connected with adolescence, dealing in great detail with conversion and religious awakening in its various phases. Like some of its predecessors, it is based on the

---

[3] Professor Leuba's rather limited reputation and influence among the reading public may be due in part to the fact that he has never put his contributions in book form. I am glad to be able to add, however, that he is now engaged in the preparation of two books, one a small volume to be entitled *The Psychological Origin and the Nature of Religion* (Constable & Company, London), the other a much larger work, whose title and publisher are not yet determined upon. I give herewith a list of his more important articles in the order in which they appeared: (Leuba, 1901, 1901a, 1901b, 1902, 1903, 1904, 1904a, 1905, 1906, 1907).

answers to several questionnaires, and is divided into two parts, first, conversion, and, second, lines of religious growth not involving conversion. One may perhaps fairly question the wisdom of Dr. Starbuck's almost implicit confidence in the questionnaire method; for the responses seem at times to have been accepted and used uncritically, and rather too much is made of figures and statistical tables. Yet it would be ungracious and unjust to throw any doubt upon the genuine value of this admirable work. It presents a mass of valuable data fairly well digested and interpreted, and is of great importance for practical as well as theoretical purposes as a careful and scholarly study of the growth of the religious consciousness. The book deserves the wide reading which it has received, and is one of the two or three most important contributions to the psychology of religion that have yet been made.[4]

Before turning from what I have called the Clark school, I should mention the foundation in May, 1904, by Dr. Hall, of a periodical for the exclusive study of the psychology of religion, the *Journal of Religious Psychology and Education.* Thus far the articles that have appeared in it have been, it must be confessed, rather disappointing. A few of them have been excellent, but very many have had but little genuinely psychological value. The issues of the *Journal,* moreover, have been but few and very far between, and it might rightly be described as being published "every little while." Although it was founded four years and a half ago, only seven numbers have thus far appeared. Between March, 1906, and September, 1907, nothing was heard of it, and in the latter month two numbers were issued in one, in the praiseworthy attempt to make up for lost time. Its chief value thus far consists in its reviews of the literature of the subject, and, most of all, in forming a centre for the encouragement of work in this new field.[5]

It may justly be said that the Clark school has contributed almost half the work of any value that has yet been done in this country on the psychology of religion. It was the first to apply empirical methods thoroughly to the study of the religious consciousness. It has collected an immense amount of data, and its chief merit, as well as its chief characteristic, is the emphasis which it has always put on the value of facts as such. As might be expected, moreover, it has the defects of its qualities. Its fondness for facts seems at times almost a blind craving. Meaning and perspective are often disregarded and forgotten in the worship of the naked fact. The apocryphal tale concerning the *Report on Child Study,* that out of eleven children who were pinched

[4] In connection with the Clark school reference should be made to three other contributions: Hylan (1901), Hall (1904), and Moses (1906).

[5] In this connection I should mention the foundation in May, 1907, of another journal in the same field and with the same object, the *Zeitschrift für Religionspsychologie,* edited by Dr. Johannes Bresler, in Halle, and appearing monthly. The articles that have thus far appeared in it pay especial attention to pathological religious phenomena. A large part of each number is devoted to excellent reviews of the literature of the subject.

14

five said, "Ouch!" and six said, "Ou!" seems quite credible to one who has read some of the writings of the Clark School. Thus from one of these (itself in many ways a valuable piece of work) I cull the following: "Stained glass windows were preferred by 149 of 175 who answered the question. Of these 19 wished pictures in them." Yet it must be said that love of facts is a good fault, especially in a young science. The psychology of religion will not be beyond the early empirical stage for some time to come, and it is a fortunate thing that in its youthful years it has been so largely formed and guided by a body of thorough-going empiricists.

But the men of the Clark school have not been the only workers in this field. Even on the subject of conversion, which has been so exhaustively studied at Worcester, some of the best work has been done by men in other parts of the country. Prominent among these are Professor George A. Coe (1900) and Mr. Luther Gulick (1897-1898). Professor Coe's book, *The Spiritual Life,* has been widely read, and has exerted a considerable influence upon the ministry, especially in the Methodist Church. It follows lines similar to those of Starbuck's *Psychology of Religion,* dealing chiefly with conversion and religious feeling; and, though without so broad an empirical basis as the latter book has, its facts are critically and safely interpreted. Like Starbuck's book, also, it is of practical as well as theoretical value, and is a useful guide to those dealing with religious problems at first hand. It is encouraging to note that these two investigators, though working quite independently of each other, have reached almost identical conclusions.

The most important single contribution to the psychology of religion is, of course, Professor James's *Varieties of Religious Experience,* first given as the Gifford Lectures at Edinburgh in 1901-1902, and later published in book form (James, 1902). Unlike most of its predecessors of which I have made mention, it is not limited to a single topic such as adolescence or conversion, but covers a great number of religious phenomena. The book is so widely read and has been so frequently reviewed that I need not comment upon it here. Like the works of the Clark school, it is thoroughly empirical in its point of view, being based chiefly, not indeed upon responses to a questionnaire, but upon biographies of religious leaders and other individuals whose religious nature has been marked and developed beyond the ordinary. Possibly it is in part the result of this that, on the one hand, the book is entirely without any of those meaningless and ill-digested accumulations of facts which sometimes mar the work of the Clark school, and that, on the other hand, a slightly distorted view of the religious consciousness has been given, much stress being laid on extreme and often abnormal cases, while the average and commonplace is negected as being uninteresting and uninstructive. Much, however, may be said for Professor James's choice of cases, as it is a well-known fact that any phenomenon can be at least more clearly made out when accentuated, and not overlaid by, nor confused with, a mass of irrelevant material. And certainly, without the assistance of his somewhat extreme types, Professor James would have had some difficulty in building up so good a case for his final thesis as he has done. For his book is not, like most of its predecessors, merely a psychological study of certain varieties of religious experience; it is, in addition to that, an attempt to see whether the facts studied may not be regarded as having some ultimate significance, and as being one way or the other on the deeper philosophical questions of religion. As everyone knows, Professor James's conclusion is that these facts are genuinely and deeply significant; that the religious view of the universe is nearer the truth than the limited view of natural science; and that we may accept it as a demonstrable truth of psychology that "the conscious person is continuous with a wider self through which saving experiences come."

Professor James's emphasis upon the importance of the marginal region of the mind is criticised in Dr. Irving King's admirable monograph, *The Differentiation of the Religious Consciousness* (1905). This work deals with religion as a social rather than as an individual product, and especially as a tribal reaction among primitive peoples.

Two more books, each dealing with a limited portion only of the general field, should perhaps be mentioned before turning from America to France; I refer to Professor Davenport's *Primitive Traits in Religious Revivals* and my own *Psychology of Religious Belief.* The former is a study of the revival from the psychological and sociological points of view; the latter an attempt to analyze religious belief and to discover its psychological bases or elements and its present strength.

The psychology of religion was born and has flourished best in America; and for the very good reason that there is so much religion here to be studied. In this country religion has not been compressed into a formal and uniform mould, as is likely to be the case in Catholic lands, nor has its emotional expression, so interesting to the psychologist, been suppressed by the proprieties and conventions of a self-conscious culture. Something, however, has been done in other countries, particularly in France, on the psychology of religion.[6] But the French psychologists, not having the advantages of the American community with its innumerable and varied living specimens close at hand, have turned to the records of the past for their material. By this I do not mean to imply that France is not a religious country, nor that it cannot furnish a great deal of valuable

---

[6] I have already referred to the German periodical of religious psychology, and if space permitted mention should here be made of the work of Vorbrodt, Kinast, Vierkandt, Braasch, and others, as well as of two or three English investigators. In neither of these countries, however, has the psychology of religion been so clearly differentiated from the philosophy of religion as is the case in America and France.

data for the psychologist. Some excellent work has in fact been done, particularly by M. Arréat (1903) on material gathered at first hand and largely by means of questionnaires, dealing with the religious consciousness in France today. But the expressions of religion in France are so stamped and colored by the forms of an ancient and firmly established ecclesiasticism that they lack the spontaneity and naturalness so prominent in the American type. Hence, as I have said, most of the French psychologists who have interested themselves in religion have sought their material in biographies rather than from questionnaires; and it is therefore in France that we find the best psychological work upon that very important phenomenon, mysticism. Innumerable treatises upon the mystics had, of course, long been compiled—treatises theological, historical, physiological—but no serious study had been made upon them from the strictly psychological point of view until the new school of psychologists of religion entered upon their work.[7] The first of these to take the field was Professor Ernest Murisier, of the Académie de Neuchâtel in Paris. In 1901 he published a book entitled *Les maladies du sentiment religieux,* which formed the starting-point for a considerable amount of genuine psychological work on the mystics. The book is devoted to a study of two kind of *maladie,* namely, an extreme type of mysticism, and fanaticism. Murisier shows that each of these abnormal phenomena is an exaggeration of a normal tendency: one, of the tendency to unify one's own personality; the other, of the impulse to social usefulness. The title of the book (together with its implications) is unfortunate, being at once too narrow and too broad, implying, as it does, that mysticism and fanaticism are the only forms of religious pathology, and, on the other hand, that all forms of mysticism are pathological. Of course there have been abnormal mystics, and Murisier's study of these is admirable; but to write down mysticism as such, at the very start, as a "maladie du sentiment religieux" is dogmatic and unempirical. If one makes allowance for these defects, however, and reads Murisier's book merely as an analysis of certain admittedly pathological phenomena, he will find it extremely illuminating. Its influence has already been very considerable, and its value as a contribution to this branch of psychology is, I believe, not merely that of a pioneer but intrinsic and permanent. It was a great misfortune to the psychology of religion that Professor Murisier, who gave such brilliant promise, died only two years after the publication of his book.

The unfortunate one-sidedness of Murisier's work on mysticism has in large part been avoided by subsequent writers on this subject—prominent among whom should be mentioned Delacroix, Godfernaux, Boutroux,

---

[7] Mention should, however, be made of Charbounier's *Maladies des mystiques* (1874), and Lejeune's *Introduction à la vie mystique* (1899), which, though not chiefly psychological in aim, contain much genuine psychology.

Leuba, and de Montmorand.[8] The best single article that has yet appeared on mysticism is probably that of Professor Leuba, "Tendances fondamentales des mystiques Chrétiens," which was published in the *Revue Philosophique* in 1902. The same emphasis on the naturalistic point of view that was seen in Leuba's other writings is here especially manifest, and great pains are taken to show that every detail of the mystic's experience can be fully accounted for in terms of physiological psychology. Yet while he resolutely rules out the transcendental, and refuses to attribute any ultimate or metaphysical significance to mysticism, Leuba is quite willing to admit its moral value, and does much greater justice to the mystics than did Murisier.

No one could put the naturalistic view of mysticism, and of religion in general, more clearly or more persuasively than Leuba has done. Yet that another point of view is possible, and that even psychologists may take it, is shown not only by Professor James's *Varieties* but by some of the writers of the French school, notably Boutroux and Flournoy. These men admit all the facts as described by the physiological psychologist, yet maintain that the facts may bear, and that some of them do bear, a philosophical significance which goes beyond the province of physiological psychology.

The psychology of religion of course does not wish to be metaphysics. It would be merely a science, descriptive and empirical, dealing frankly with phenomena, and ranking merely as a branch of general psychology. As such it collects data, compiles statistics, makes comparisons, and seeks to pass from the level of mere facts to classifications, generalizations, and laws. It is with this aim in view that it has made use of purely empirical methods and has sought to formulate its results in purely psychological and physiological terms. Whether it has always been successful in these efforts is indeed somewhat dubious. Its use of the questionnaire method has frequently been uncritical, and its physiological phraseology and fanciful explanations of complex states by diagraphs of nerve-paths seem often an attempt at too great simplification; sometimes they impress one as positively ridiculous. Yet, though it has not fully learned the use of its tools, it has maintained with fair consistency a just notion of its proper aim—namely, to discover the facts, and to describe, classify, and explain them.

While all this is true, however, and while every reference to anything "supernatural" is rightly barred out from psychology as a natural science, it might conceivably be found that the facts as collected and described could best be explained and accounted for on some hypothesis other than the somewhat naïve naturalism adopted by the majority of scientists. It

[8] Delacroix's book is entitled *Études d'histoire et de psychologie du mysticisme* (1908). It is not only the latest, but the most elaborate and exhaustive, treatment of the subject.

Boutroux's work appeared in the *Bulletin de l'Institut Psychol. Int.*, that of the others in the *Revue Philosophique*, between 1902 and 1905.—I make no mention here of the work of Binet-Sanglé, as it deals almost exclusively with the psychological side of religion.

might, for example, turn out that the data in hand pointed toward some such hypothesis as that of Professor James—a "wider self" or psychic "beyond," in touch with the subconscious portion of our lives. If further investigations continued to point more and more in this direction, and new evidence for the existence of such a "beyond" were forthcoming, new facts which seemed best explicable on such a supposition, this hypothesis would have to be regarded as a perfectly scientific one, and the "beyond" would not be something supernatural but just one of the regular facts of nature, like the western hemisphere or the process of digestion or the state of hypnosis. The scientist sees nothing supernatural in the luminiferous ether, and he believes in its existence because of certain facts, which indeed might conceivably be otherwise explained, but which seem most simply and fully explicable on that hypothesis. So it might very well be with the psychological hypothesis in question. To maintain that such an hypothesis is *"grundsätzlich ausgeschlossen,"* that it is *impossible* because "unscientific," is dogmatic and unempirical, and is an utterly unwarranted playing into the hands of a crude and shallow materialism. It is forgotten that naturalism of this kind involves a metaphysic quite as truly as does idealism.

And much indeed may be said for such a non-naturalistic explanation. There are certain facts connected with mysticism and the religious consciousness which seem to point in that general direction. The naturalistic school has still a great deal to do before it can prove its hypothesis the only tenable one. In a sense, to be sure, it can explain all the facts of the religious consciousness, just as the Ptolemaic theory can be made to explain all the movements of the heavenly bodies. The question still remains, Is it the best explanation? Until more data have come in, the naturalistic and what I may call the religious hypotheses must run along parallel with each other as rival alternatives. And so long as science looks to experience as its guide and remains genuinely empirical, the truly scientific man will keep an open mind, and though he may believe one of the alternatives to be false, will remember that further experience may show him to be mistaken, and hence that it behooves him, in the present state of our ignorance, to avoid dogmatism on either side of the controversy.

The question, then, is still an open one. But, on the other hand, we must not forget that the naturalistic hypothesis has proved itself most useful and fruitful in results in all fields in which it has been consistently applied— something which can hardly be said for its rival, which has only too often, in the hands of over-enthusiastic and uncritical supporters, proved a stumbling-block to genuine scientific progress. And it must be admitted, moreover, that while the religious hypothesis has by no means been disproved, it is still far from showing itself indisputably and clearly the best explanation. It is still, like its rival, merely one of two possible alternatives. So long as this is the case, it would seem best for the psychologist, *as psycholo-*

gist, to work along the lines laid down by the naturalistic hypothesis, and to seek to explain all the facts so far as possible by means of the laws already clearly established by physiological psychology. If he doubts their sufficiency to explain everything, let him subject them to the test of universal application; for, if they are really inadequate and in need of supplementation, their insufficiency can be shown in no better way. This he should do, I say, as a psychologist; but this in no wise hinders him from holding to whatever transcendental explanation he may, as a religious man or as a philosopher, deem most satisfactory. An idealistic universe may be large enough to embrace a naturalistic science. And while we are still uncertain as to the proper explanation of our facts, the many data of psychology which seem to point toward a religious interpretation of the world, even though they fit in with a naturalistic description, may very properly combine with one's otherwise grounded religious outlook or idealistic philosophy to justify one, *as a man,* in holding to such a belief.

There is, therefore, nothing to hinder the psychology of religion from furnishing philosophy with material which it can use in support of a religious view of reality; and there is much in the recent investigations of the religious consciousness which may well strengthen the faith of the religious man. But it is not merely on the theoretical side that the new science can be of use to religion. In fact the practical religious worker will gain quite as much assistance from this branch of investigation as will the philosopher or the theologian. The recent elaborate and exact studies in the religion of childhood, the phenomena of adolescence, the nature of conversion and the age at which it is to be expected, and in several other related subjects, cannot fail to be of value to the intelligent pastor, teacher, and parent. And in a more general sense the psychology of religion should be of considerable practical assistance to all those who are seriously studying the larger tendencies of the times and earnestly seeking to contribute their share toward the wise guidance of the community in its religious life.

There is a growing feeling, shared by most close students of the times, that we are in the midst of a serious religious crisis. The almost universal acceptance of biological evolution, the higher criticism of the Scriptures, the naturalistic trend of modern science, and the general increasing demand for independence of thought, are bringing about their inevitable results. The old authorities and the old arguments for the religious view of the world are yearly, even daily, losing their hold over the community. Views which would have been considered downright heresy twenty-five years ago are taught in most of our colleges and theological seminaries and openly preached from our pulpits. Side by side with this intellectual change has come a falling off in church attendance and a loss of prestige on the part of the church in general. And so the question inevitably forces itself upon every serious observer who has the interests of the community and the race at heart, whether religion, if it is to last, must not give up her time-honored trust in the old authorities and seek to draw most or all of her strength from some other quarter.

In trying to answer this vitally serious question we must avail ourselves of every means in our power to see the situation exactly as it is. What, in short, is the real strength of religion in the community? And here we have a right to look for assistance to the psychology of religion. As yet, indeed, but little has been done toward answering this question; but the task of feeling the pulse of the religious community and investigating the real nature and strength of its religious belief naturally belongs to religious psychology, and, though vast, is well worth its while. An interesting investigation with a somewhat similar aim has just been concluded by the *Mecure de France*,[9] which, though hardly belonging to psychology in the stricter sense of the word, furnishes rich material to the psychologist, and possibly throws some light upon the problem just referred to. The following question was sent out to a number of the leaders of thought throughout Europe: "Are we passing through a dissolution, or an evolution, of religious ideas and of the religious sentiment?" To this question over one hundred and twenty-five answers were received, of which about twenty maintained that religion is destined to dissolution, while a hundred or more insisted that it is imperishable. Of course a mere collection of opinions such as this touches only the surface of the problem. A more thoroughgoing investigation and one more psychological in its nature is that of M. Arréat in the book referred to a few pages back, *Le sentiment religieux en France*. After a careful consideration of the facts at hand, Arréat reaches the conclusion that "France has ceased to be passionately Catholic," and that there is no reason to believe it will ever become Protestant. "The Frenchman gives up the religion of his fathers to turn to scepticism or some philosophy." But, as the writer points out, this philosophy, and even this scepticism, may be, if not essentially Christian, at least throughly religious. For the man who is naturally religious will remain so, no matter what his creed; and religious belief is not confined to what we call either Catholicism or Protestantism. For all who desire to inform themselves on the religious condition of France today Arréat's book is invaluable; and investigations of a similar nature in England, Germany, and this country are a decided desideratum.[10] If the study were seriously undertaken by a number of capable investigators and a much greater body of data collected than Arréat was able to gather, it would fur-

[9] See the numbers for April 15, May 1 and 15, June 1 and 15, and July 1, 1907. Professor Goblet d'Alviella has published a brief summary of the investigation in the *Revue de Belgique*, which was reproduced in translation in the *Open Court* for January, 1908.

[10] Something of the sort has of course been done by a number of writers: cf. Shailer Mathews's *The Church and the Changing Order*, and Dr. Broda's review of the religious situation the world over in the *International* for March, 1908.

nish us with some very serviceable information as to the real status of religious belief and feeling. We can hardly steer our course wisely and successfully unless we know with some approximate degree of exactness just
where we are.

There is, however, something of vastly greater importance and usefulness in this matter than statistics, and that is a knowledge of the real nature
of religion and of the religious consciousness in general. From what region
of man's nature does religion chiefly spring? Where are its strongest in-
trenchments? If the old authoritative foundations be shaken, is there really
any other base to which religion may safely turn? These are, after all, the
important questions, and upon them the psychology of religion can speak
with authority and with no uncertain voice.

For with almost complete unanimity the workers in this field maintain
that religion is a matter of temperament and attitude and demand rather
than one of creed and intellectual belief. With this temperament as a basis
of division, it may be said that every community is roughly divisible into
two classes of people, the religious and the non-religious. The former is
probably the larger of the two—in fact, it seems probable that, in this country
at least, more people are naturally religious than is generally supposed; we
Anglo-Saxons are, on the whole, more likely to hide our deeper feelings
than to parade them. Yet it must be confessed that we cannot tell with
any exactness the relative size of the two classes. Church statistics certainly
throw very little light upon it. For while some of the non-religious class
call themselves "sceptics," the majority of them are to be found within
the churches. These people have never been religious, and perhaps never
can be. Religion has never taken any real hold upon them, and if they believe in God, it is in the same abstract way in which they believe in the Czar
of Russia or the binomial theorem. The loss of this belief would indeed
result in their ceasing to class themselves as Christians, and might even for a
time decrease their respect for morality by removing from them certain
traditional restraints and sanctions. We ought therefore to hesitate indeed
before shaking their faith in the old authorities. And yet even should this
be done—gradually and after a time—we should have no reason to anticipate
any very serious results. New abstract beliefs would soon replace the old
ones; new moral sanctions would take up the functions of those laid aside;
and the individuals themselves, never having known the spiritual life, would
suffer no great loss, being quite as religious after the change of creed as before it.

The class of people who are religious, like those who are not, are also
found both within the church and without it, among the believers and
among the sceptics. They are, of course, of various types, differing both in
the kind and in the intensity of their feelings and beliefs. With some the
"mystic germ" has been but slightly developed, being a demand or yearning

rather than an intuition or an emotional certainty. With some the question of creed is of considerably more importance than with others, and in their case the overthrow of an old doctrine may work serious loss. But for the great majority a creed is but an external thing; and the rejection of one or the adoption of another, though it may mean temporary pain and struggle, is in the long run but an incidental matter. For, as I have said, nearly all the students of this subject in our day as well as in the past agree that religion in its genuine form grows out of the emotional rather than the intellectual nature, or, better still, from the man as a whole, and that the overthrow of an authority or the refutation of an argument has but little permanent effect upon the really religious spirit. In the case of the great majority of what I have called the religious class, underneath the externals of creed and cult, deep down in the hidden recesses of the conscious life, there flows a stream of religious intuitions and demands which are vital and almost instinctive in their nature, and which refuse to be utterly abolished or destroyed by anything that science or criticism can do. Religion is a more vital thing than science; it goes down deeper into life than does any intellectual doctrine: hence its forms and expressions, its creed and its liturgies, may indeed be altered and destroyed; but through all these changes the essential part of the religious nature remains itself unchanged, serenely defying the power of successive scientific dogmas and shifting "psychological atmospheres." It is an easy thing to pick a few leaves from an ancient oak—a child may do it, and when he has done so new leaves will grow again; but to pluck up the oak with all its deep-lying and branching roots—that would be a task that might well prove too much for the strength even of a giant.

An illustration of the vitality of religion after most of its usual modes of expression have been given up is seen in that not uncommon phenomenon, the religious agnostic. It happens not infrequently that men of culture and intellectual power, well versed in the science and criticism of our day, feel themselves unable to subscribe to any creed or to worship with any church, yet find springing up within them a stream of inarticulate but genuine religious experience and intuition which is to them the very water of life. At the risk of proving tedious, let me quote from one such instance, the confession of a French agnostic:

"I seem to feel within the depths of my being an action, a presence; in short, I seem to be the object, even prior to being the subject, of an action that is spiritual. This is in part a rudimentary, half-conscious belief, in part it is simply the expression of a fact, the testimony to a sort of profound and vague sensation. I tell myself that this sensation itself may be an illusion, that there may be nothing real about it apart from my subjectivity; but it *is,* and that is enough for me to live by. . . . It is a part of my being, and has for the rest of my being an importance and a value that are supreme— that suffices me. And for the rest, I tell myself that the very fact that I possess this experience called 'religious' is a witness in me to the existence of the inaccessible reality; of the union, within my consciousness, of the me and the not-me; that in it I have in some measure an immediate knowledge of the roots of my being, of a bond between me and something else, this 'something else' being necessarily self-conscious since it passes within my self-consciousness. . . . And just because I have become agnostic, and because every intellectual formulation of the inaccessible is for me simply a representation of the Reality, without any value in itself, I feel myself on solid ground. I have the experience there within that I have not to act but to receive; that I have not the initiative but the duty of waiting and listening; that the source of life is beyond the conscious self, for me, for all men." [11]

This man is perfectly capable of taking the naturalistic point of view, of looking at his religious experience objectively and seeing that it might be classified as hallucinatory. And yet the experience loses none of its authority, none of its certainty, for him. The naturalistic interpretation he deems quite consistent and tenable; yet for his own part he is convinced that the religious explanation is the true one, and his agnosticism on all points of creed and theology in no wise interferes. He remains a religious man spite of his agnosticism, because this religious experience of his is his very own, and because it has for his life a value that is supreme. And this suggests two important considerations which deserve brief mention here.

The authority of the religious intuition, the "mystic germ," is seldom or never questioned. As in the case just quoted, this inner experience of the man himself seems inevitably, and in spite of rival and plausible interpretations, to claim for itself an unfaltering credence which no intellectual belief, gained by painstaking induction or labored reasoning or external authority, can ever enjoy. And, secondly, if it ever comes to a matter of argumentation at all—which in fact is seldom the case—there is one argument in favor of the acceptance of this inner experience at its face value which, to him who has known it, is usually quite decisive; namely, *its value for life*. In the words of our agnostic friend, it is "enough to live by," "it is a part of my being, and has for the rest of my being an importance and a value that are supreme, and that suffices me." We outsiders may classify it learnedly as "phénomène hallucinatoire"; but the man himself knows that it is good to live by, life-giving—and "cela me suffit." This fact of the value of religion for life is attested alike by the psychology and the history of religion and by the experience of the common man. And until human nature gets radically changed, it would seem that man will remain a religious creature, quite irrespective of the rise and fall of any dogmas, be they theological or scientific.

Of course there is nothing essentially new in all this. Yet it will hardly seem superfluous to have a belief long held on the authority of the intuition

[11] Quoted from Flournoy, who reports the case in length.

of a few confirmed by a painstaking and systematic study of a large body of facts carefully and critically collected and sifted. And in throwing more light upon the essential nature of the religious consciousness, the psychology of religion has contributed something of genuine value for the guidance of all who are trying to deal with the present crisis wisely and well.

The Psychology of Religion

E. L. Schaub

THE PUBLICATIONS SINCE 1920 ON THE PSYCHOLOGY OF RELIGION ARE SO NU-merous and so varied that any brief survey of them must necessarily re-strict, with more or less arbitrariness, the field of its attention. Although psychologists of religion may glean much from certain portrayals of con-crete experiences furnished by biographies and historical studies, this litera-ture must here be left uncited. We shall also omit studies of magic and of primitive culture generally, along with publications that might be claimed by anthropology, sociology or history, and a vast literature that is decidedly popular or scientifically inferior. With this mere mention we pass the rich material in the eleventh and twelfth volumes of the *Encyclopedia of Religion and Ethics* and in the *Dictionary of Religion and Ethics*. As to the broad field of religious mysticism and the literature essentially Freudian in method, they have been sundered out for treatment by others in special articles (Cronbach, 1926; Leuba, 1926). Despite all these restrictions and omissions, that which still remains for our presentation is so vast in amount and in range of method, problem, and conclusion as to permit of but the most hurried notice.

The period under our consideration has brought to a close the earnest work of Girgensohn (1921, 1923, 1924).[1] He early became convinced that it was not through investigations of historical persons or phenomena but alone

From "The Psychology of Religion," *Psychological Bulletin,* 23 (1926), 681-700. Used by per-mission of American Psychological Association.

[1] Girgensohn died at the age of fifty on September 20, 1925. First a professor in Greifswald, he later transferred to Leipzig.

through the study of living individuals that the psychology of religion could enjoy a healthy scientific growth. His touch with American publications, however, left him with a belief that real advance would depend upon the discovery of an experimental method that would bring to light material of whose existence the experiencer himself had previously been not at all, or but very dimly, aware. The psychoanalytic methods met this condition but they seemed unsatisfactory on other counts. Such being the case, Girgensohn was challenged by the work of Marbe, Watt, Messer, Buehler, and Ach—by their method of systematic introspection under controlled conditions, as well as by their discovery of elusive and unintuitable material and functions of consciousness. For his guide he turned to Kuelpe. The latter's influence in this field had already extended to the *Nuernberger Arbeitsgemeinschaft fuer Religionspsychologie,* in whose organ, *Archiv fuer Religionspsychologie,* W. Staehlin, in 1914, published the first article inspired by the new method.

Girgensohn selected a number of very different religious poems, both familiar and unfamiliar, and set his highly trained observers the task of expressing a judgment as to their worth after a single reading made in as natural a manner as possible. At the outset, the observers were asked to give both objective and subjective evaluations, but this distinction was later dropped. Indeed, it gradually also seemed advisable to ask merely in general for the experiences of the observers. In short, the details of the method were constantly revised in the course of the work. But into this we may not further enter. Reports were received also of experiences when the poems were read under such conditions as to permit the emergence of free associations. Through a carefully prepared direct questioning of the observers regarding the details of their reports, and through verbal attacks upon them, replies were elicited which afforded added insight into the bases of the observer's faith. To learn more fully the nature of religious trust, trained introspectionists were asked to call to mind individuals in whom they had trust and then to describe the various elements and relations discoverable in the experience. Again, the observers were asked to turn their thought upon concepts selected from the catechism, maintaining the same attitude as though in school. Kuelpe had recommended also the immediate recording of spontaneous experiences, as these might from time to time arise, the thought being that this would supplement the material obtainable through introspection under experimental conditions.

In the form in which it had been first employed in the general field of psychology, this method suffered attacks from Wundt. Not unnaturally Girgensohn's particular use of it likewise became a target for criticism (see, e.g., Spranger, 1925, p. 299n). Behn (1923), however, has reemphasized the value of introspection, insisting that self-observation is the most receptive of all thought processes, neither creating nor altering its contents (nor dealing with simply revived experiences) but reporting them as they are, without judgment upon them or apprehension of their laws; likewise he stresses the added value that accrues from experimental safeguards. Again, it was asked whether the fruits were such as to validate the method. What contributions accrued from Girgensohn's heavy labors as recorded in a volume of over seven hundred closely printed pages, many of them in small type? A partial answer may be provisionally suggested by introducing at this point some recent work by Starbuck and one of his students, E. Leigh Mudge.

Starbuck (1921) sharply demarcates the so-called higher senses, such as sight and hearing, from the "intimate" senses, such as the organic senses and the warm and cold mechanisms. According to him, the former are peculiarly apt to define their objects, to give them specific spatial and temporal settings, and to relate them more or less schematically to other objects. Their part in the deeper and riper religious experiences, however, he finds to be quite subordinate. It is the "intimate" senses that here play the central role. Their findings, though in one sense private, are truly sharable; in their reference and their validity they are as consistently objective as are the "defining" senses. They afford a direct, immediate experience of their objects; and they are indispensably involved in the process of bodily and social adjustment. They are the "sources of wisdom," of meaning and value, in religious, as in ethical and aesthetic, experience. Religion has acquired a peculiar adeptness in arousing the "intimate" senses and for this reason it has been so well able to propagate itself. In his doctoral dissertation on the God-experience, Mudge (1923) has found a field for the application and the confirmation of this general doctrine.

Now as regards the relative role of the particular kinds of sense experience in religion, Girgensohn's results had been very much the same. Though he had noted significant differences as between individuals, he nevertheless discovered that the kinaesthetic material was more regularly present than any other—indeed, that it alone was in every case to be found—and that it was never marginal, as were, for example, visual and other data. On the other hand, it became apparent to him that experiences differ greatly, ranging from the concrete to the abstract, from those in which sense data bulk large to those essentially non-presentational. Moreover, he concluded that a rigid analysis of any concrete, complex religious experience would show that no sort of sense material, presentation, or image is really more than secondary. More basic is some activity or function—some distinctive content quite other than that of either the "defining" or the "intimate" senses. The latter disclose themselves as the vehicles of what is non-presentational. They are essentially symbolic in character. Hence, though in themselves apparently enigmatic or absurd, they may yet indicate a meaning worthy of search. Feelings of pleasure or displeasure, too, are subordinate. Bliss and joy are mere accompaniments. Much the same may be said of the volitional processes.

27

In religion they are indeed aroused. Conversion, for example, reaches its consummation only with a dedication of the will. Yet conversion itself depends upon deep-lying processes which alone enable the will to exercise itself with freedom in the direction of religious realization. The volitional functions, thus, are not primary; they are symptoms, as it were, of an inner change; they are the active expressions of a new life. The real and ultimate secret of religion is to be found in a new attitude of the ego such as arises without a consciousness of freedom. The core of religion is an intuitively entertained God-consciousness and a characteristic relation or attitude of the self thereto. As regards the latter, there is an alternation between an intensified self-feeling, wherein the ego is expansive and beautiful through the indwelling of the divine, and a diminished or annulled self-feeling, in which the boundary between the Ego and the Other has faded or disappeared. In a long section devoted to a comparison of his results with what one finds in the accounts given by mystics, Girgensohn finds a remarkable harmony. That is, in his view ordinary religious experiences include, at least marginally or in some degree, the features long known to characterize mysticism. One finds in them tendencies towards a lapse of the consciousness of time and space; the experience of thoughts and feelings as not one's own but as those of another who, however, is yet not demarcated from one's self; the dedication of one's self to a being that is greater and is yet valued as one's very own.

For Wobbermin (1921, 1925) also every exclusively observational or strictly objective empiricism stands condemned; the nature of religion discloses itself only from within the experience itself. To overcome sheer subjectivism, however, the individual must, through an act of imagination, put himself in the very midst of forms of religious life other than his own. Utilizing his personal inner life as a key, he must especially attempt to get at the core of the major historical religions. Thus will his own perception of religion's nature be refined and his power increased of discriminating the truly universal features of his own experience. The method of Wobbermin thus involves creative empathy and a *religionspsychologischer Zirkel*. Since this method empowers one to distinguish the accidental, transitory, and subjective from the central and permanent features of the experience, and thus leads to a definition of what religion truly is, Wobbermin has described it as transcendental. The view of religion to which it leads is that of "a relationship of man to an overworld in which he believes and in belief foreknows, on which he feels himself dependent, in whose shelter he knows himself to be secure and which is the goal of his heart's most ardent yearning" (1921, p. 254).

Hoeffding's monograph (1923), though bringing out the psychological and epistemological relations between experience and interpretation, nevertheless follows the path of his earlier *Philosophy of Religion* in definitely sundering them. A comparative study of mystical phenomena of different

28

types and periods leads him to the conclusion that personal experience has acquired a constantly increasing importance and independence until we of today tend to hold that nothing that does not spring from it is of religious value. Now it is experience which Wobbermin also stresses. He, however, thinks of it as including ideas and interpretation. Psychologically, he contends, religious experience incorporates an element of conviction, as well as some formulation thereof in ideational or even rational terms; also imagery of various sorts, distinguishable as primary and secondary. The ideational and imaginal constituents are, to be sure, strongly dominated by social influences; yet the experience as a whole, he holds, is essentially individual rather than social in character.

Winkler (1921) belongs to those who believe that every strictly psychological approach is hopelessly inadequate because in every form, as even in that of Wobbermin, it retains vestiges of subjectivism. Recourse is therefore taken to the phenomenological method, as this has been developed in general more especially by Husserl and his school. So also Stavenhagen (1925). He argues that every empirical account of religion, whether psychological, historical, or sociological, *presupposes* some conception by the use of which the particular set of facts studied is delimited from those which are left to one side as non-religious. Such being the case, this presupposed conception must be attained by *a priori* methods. Through reflective intuition one must and one may arrive at absolute and ontological truths, whether the materials that furnish the starting points and the cues are drawings or figures, as in the case of geometry, or personal experiences as in the case of religion. In both cases alike we may, through Wesensschau, penetrate from and through empirical data to universal, objective, ultimate features or essences. It is only thus (and not, for example, by an alternation between the inner experience of the individual and the soul of another or of an historical religion, as Wobbermin had argued) that we may escape from subjectivism to rationality. Religion is then seen to be a personal attitude that is absolute in its character. Its two main types culminate in (a) *Ehrfurchtsreligion,* in which the individual is conscious of his absolute nothingness in relation to a divine being absolutely unapproachable in the character of *tremenda majestas,* and (b) *Liebesreligion,* characterized by a consciousness of absolute at-homeness and security *(Geborgesein)* and by an object or noema representing the absolutely paternal. The fusion of these two types, in so far as attainable, yields the highest form of religion.

Spranger (1925) is thoroughly alive to the force of the contention that the psychology of religion must look to non-psychological methods for that conception or definition of religion without which it cannot intelligently get under way. He realizes the great difficulty, if not the sheer impossibility, of completely sundering considerations of validity and of relative worth from psychological description. Nevertheless he holds that the latter may safely

29

proceed in practical independence of the former provided it guards against narrowness of outlook and takes under observation primitive, undeveloped, and degenerate forms of "religion," and also phenomena but partially "religious." While in so far subscribing to a strictly empirical method, he is conscious of the limitations of the questionnaire, of diaries, or of the experimentally controlled introspections secured by Girgensohn. Superior, in his view, is the procedure of Bohne (1922) who enriched our knowledge of adolescent religious development through the use of autobiographical materials. Spranger refers with appreciation to an essay in a memorial volume dedicated to Max Weber in which Hans Gruhle discusses autobiography as a source of historical knowledge. In autobiographies personal contacts loom large, and it is through these, more especially, that religion is kindled and nourished.

Thus holding, Spranger is critical also of the method employed by Dehn (1923) in determining the religious outlook of the proletarian youth. To the latter Dehn presented as themes for essays three words so selected that, though in a way unconnected, they could readily be brought into meaningful relations. Examples are: God-Help-Death, God-Worship-Nature, God-Freedom-Fatherland. But, Spranger urges, does not each of these sets of words inevitably suggest certain lines of thought, and may not the latter, even as followed in the essay, be an expression of tradition or the social environment rather than of the living experience of the youth? And do we not thus get at best some idea of their relation to the Church and to ecclesiastical Christianity rather than of their ultimate, life-satisfying values? In part, Dehn himself realized this. So in drawing his conclusions he refrained from taking into consideration many of the essays or *Selbstzeugnisse* on the ground that they clearly bore the earmarks of traditional thought, of a perfunctory fulfilment of an essay or school requirement, of a literary group, or of sheer imagination. In the 2,400 essays received, Dehn found abundant evidence that the proletarian youth lean heavily upon the authority of what they daily hear; they think as proletarians and thus discard Christianity and all transcendent beliefs; they reflect a stage of disintegration in which, however, there are surviving traces of the past, especially in respect to various age-old ceremonials connected with crises in life, as, for example, baptism, dedication, wedding, burial.

If we further adhere to methodology as our primary guiding thread in presenting some connected account of the more important recent work in the psychology of religion, we may next refer to three American writers. Stratton (1923) has published another significant study of the spirit revealed in the sacred writings of the more developed religions, presenting in this instance, partly through a disclosure of contrasts and antitheses, the role therein of anger. The book is both interesting and valuable, though it suffers from a failure to distinguish anger from its compounds, from its sublimations and from related emotions. The concluding section insists on "both the possibility and the need of bringing our anger-responses into the service of the interests that deserve to be supreme, and in particular of making pugnacity obedient to good-will." Leuba (1921), through a new publisher, has brought out a second edition of his *The Belief in God and Immortality*. This study represents pioneer work in the application of statistical methods to the subject of religious beliefs; it brings out forcibly the differences, as respects both origin and function, between an earlier or primary conception of survival after death and that which later took form; and it contends for the essential independence of morality as respects the religious beliefs under discussion. Starbuck (as appears in the printed outlines of his Oslo lectures) has essayed the task of securing correlations exhibiting evaluations, singly and collectively, of the interacting elements in combinations of relations, as, *e.g.*, in the case of "conservatives" as distinguished from "radicals" and of the "mystical" as distinguished from the "practical-minded" types in religion. Butler (1921), we might here inject, has pointed out that the ecclesiastical historian would be greatly aided if psychologists would throw light on the religious genius and his influence through a study of contemporary leaders who are winning converts.

Combining the historical approach with psychological analysis, Delacroix (1922) has set forth the main types of religious faith and their connected experiences, describing both their structure and their evolution. He distinguishes three types: implicit or authoritative, reasoning, and trusting faith. Into correspondence therewith he places institution, reason and sentiment, all three of which he deems essential to religion. Desire is involved: it leads to belief in the realization of its end. Also subconscious emotion: it confers upon the object the quality of transcendence. Also thought: it is represented by belief in an objective order of forces or powers. From desire and belief spring ritual, whence comes the more or less independent myth and later the dogma. Thought moves from the primitive conception of a diffused impersonal force to deities that become progressively individualized, only to be absorbed into an anonymous, infinite being. Dogma, arising from the effort of faith to understand itself, first lays claim to explanatory significance and then becomes mystery.

Hofmann (1925)—as likewise Hirsch (1922)—contends that religion is essentially an experience of salvation. The feeling of dependence, so often stressed as the essence of religion, is for him characteristic only of religious need and thus of the initial, or the negative, stage of the total experience. Succeeding it is a new feeling and attitude wherein experience acquires a positive emotional value—the stage of salvation. This may come through an alternation in one's estimation of the environing order; or, through a changed orientation in one's demands and desires; or, through a realization that one's weal is not dependent upon the external order and a conviction that one has adequate inner resources for the longed for bliss. In each of these cases there are sub-types. For example, there is self-salvation through the denial of but also through the dominance over the world. Spranger similarly describes religion as a quest for the central and total meaning of life and personality in its deeper relations with the world. Studying adolescence he concludes that this is not a collection of unrelated tendencies but a striving for a total meaning, in the various phases of which we have a "reflection of the divine in the soul and an irradiation of the discovered God into the world" (1925, p. 326).

Continuing with Spranger, it should be noted that in his discussion he treats separately religious development (a) within a moderate religious atmosphere, (b) within an intense religious atmosphere, and (c) within an atmosphere religiously indifferent or hostile, at least in the Christian sense of these terms. Clavier (1926) has made careful observations regarding the ideas of God among children. Discussing the religious sentiment more generally, Bovet (1925) has set forth in an original manner a thesis once enunciated by G. Stanley Hall to the effect that love towards God is a development of filial love. As regards both the moral and the mystical or emotional aspects of religion, Bovet holds that children are capable of amazingly lofty experiences, bizarre as may be their ideas of God.

Regarding prayer as the central phenomenon of religion, Heiler (1923) has devoted to its interpretation an enormous volume that strikingly exhibits the typical German scholar's delight in thoroughness and completeness as regards detail, distinctions, and bibliographical references. A lucid essay designed more especially "to dispute the negative conclusion of some psychological and psycho-analytical theories regarding the objective validity of—the prayer-life" has been contributed by Relton (see Hardman, 1925). The book by Stolz (1923) must be classed not among the contributions to science but among the efforts to assist thoughtful people "in the discovery of those prayer values which will further adjustment to the expanding universe of to-day."

Pratt (1920) has urged the importance of distinguishing two types of conversion: the emotional type and that in which the center of the struggle is life's chief values and something much more objective is sought than a mere emotional change. Langley (1924) insists that the marked changes in attitude that characterize the "genuine" experience remain inadequately explained if we keep to the standpoint of inherited conative processes functioning within empirically observable situations. Lutoslawski (1923) writes of (a) superficial conversion—exemplified by most revival cases, explicable by external suggestion of some sort, and short-lived—and (b) genuine conversion. The latter shows individual characteristics differing in particular cases. It is fairly enduring in its effects. Moreover, it is explicable only by reference to a higher Power, for while a certain preparation is a necessary precondition this is not its real cause. To understand such conversion, therefore, we do better to study its consequences than its causes. Northridge (1924) reaches parallel conclusions in his discussion of the types of evangelism.

On the basis of reports from Protestant missionaries, Allier (1925) has written of conversion as this takes place in connection with missionary work among uncivilized peoples. Three divisions of the treatise deal with preliminary steps to conversion, the conversion crisis, and consequences which follow the crisis.

Baillie (1926) holds that "when you get behind religious ideas, you also, and by the same sign, get behind religious feelings;" that the sentimentalist, mystical and experience theologies (the three varieties of romanticism), in endeavoring to escape the absurdities of rationalism, fall into a similar pit; that no "interpretation of religion can be worthy of its great object . . . which does not exhibit it as a thing born of, and nourished by, the fullest daylight of human intelligence." Brotherston (1924), on the other hand, accepts a directive or formative impulse which, not deposited by experience but included in man's instinctive equipment, progressively asserts itself by way of governing the specific instincts and thus effecting a unification of life. At times we are reminded of Marshall's *Instinct and Reason*. Yet man's instinctive equipment is further described as "interrelated part with part and unified within the scope of one most general instinct," and this is obviously in acceptance of Hocking (1918) to whom indeed Brotherston himself refers. Lidgett (1923) argues that the various instincts and affections *"as experienced* are partial manifestations of, and *as intellectually represented* are abstractions from, a spiritual potentiality which, though undeveloped at the outset, contains within itself the promise of the religious sentiment. When ultimately this sentiment is developed it gains the power, not only of transcending the whole content of human affections from which it has become differentiated, but of returning to control and organize into a higher unity all the affective elements which for the ordinary purposes of human life have been drawn off from the central stream of spiritual life." Very different indeed is the portrayal of religion in terms of that conception of sentiment, which we owe primarily to Shand and McDougall. Such a description and the resulting doctrines represent the most valuable part of the psychological section of Wright's book (1922); and in a recent paper (Wright, 1924) the same writer has further refined his analysis and has indicated the resulting psychological definitions of righteousness, temptation, sin, repentance, forgiveness, atonement, grace, etc.

Shailer Mathews (1923) has put theology within the setting of social psychology. In distinction from philosophy, which is an unofficial and an individual interpretation, theology, he believes, is an expression of group belief, and its meanings must therefore be sought by reference to social origins.

33

For it is derived from customs and ritual which antedate doctrines and, not strangely, its terms are social "patterns." It is therefore functional in nature, and the value of its formulas must be determined by reference to whether or not they promote the group life. Sacraments are treated from a similar functional and genetic viewpoint by Cooke (1924). Such also, of course, has been Ames's approach, leading to his conception of religion as "the consciousness of the highest social values." This definition has been sharply criticized by Pratt (1920, pp. 8ff) on the ground that it identifies religion with social righteousness. Leuba (1912) has also warned against the identification of religion with moral or social devotion. Are there not important psychological differences in attitude between adherents of organized religious and devoted atheistical servants of society? Ames (1921) has replied that by "consciousness" (in his definition) he means both appreciation and the active attitude of supporting, and by "highest" the most intimate and vital phases of the social consciousness, these phases, of course, being relative to the social group. And, he asks, has not religion in our modern age become identical with social idealism and with morality? He declares himself ready to include in his account of religion—as does Pratt—an attitude toward an ultimate Determiner of Destiny, provided only some specific empirical content be given this expression. Indeed this content varies. It may be rice, corn, bear, sheep, God in the form of a man or a king, or many another thing. But "whatever the symbol, the substance of the idea of God, the objective reality, is the Spirit of the group whose awesome will is enforced through the commandments of social custom." To the charge that this implies subjectivism and mere idea-ism, Ames retorts: "Is Alma Mater a mere idea of fiction? Is it subjective? Has it not all the reality of buildings, faculties, donors, students, etc." In a later paper he argues similarly that "when the idea of God is employed it implies a particular organization of reality in terms of the felt values of experience."

These contentions, reminiscent, among other thinkers, of Comte and Hatorp, have evoked a number of noteworthy responses. To Baillie (1926) they suggest by reaction the very point at which religion, as he believes, carries one beyond a purely humanistic or social attitude. This "something more" he finds in the assurance that in our finest social attitudes and moral endeavors "we somehow have the very Heart and Soul of things with us and are aligning ourselves with the Eternal. . . . The highest outlook and attitude are those which take our values, not as inventions, but rather as revelations, as our best and most veridical clues to the nature of the System to which we belong; as representing not merely our purposes but the Universe's Purpose for us; as being not merely a meaning which we import into our lives, but rather a meaning which we find in them."

Very penetratingly Hocking (1921) has argued that the group spirit is not even for practical purposes equivalent to God. Our present society is not an organism, nor is it ideal; it is only progressing toward such; from its demands upon the individual, its powers and enforcements, there is always, factually or potentially, an appeal to another spirit. Thus the spirit of one's social order is never absolute. It is at best somewhat external, undiscerning, and lacking in appreciation and understanding of the moral and spiritual needs of the individual. In respect to the vicissitudes and experiences of the latter it is the function of God "to do better" than the social group of which the individual is a member. Again, "if there be in the universe an object upon which there can be reliance *without criticism,* a *valid* object of worship, and a source of *peace,* that object must be other than the social good." Further, "perhaps the most practical of all religious functions has been its function of assuring individual minds that they may and should aspire without limit; that in the real world the will is completely free. But if religion is to do this, it must involve the whole sweep of the objects of the mind that worships, and not any finite part of them. But the social spirit is a very finite portion of the cosmos." The argument is strengthened by reference to the fact that in religion "the worshipper seeks response and one that is individual" and by reference also to salient features of the course of religion's development. A fundamental difficulty from which we constantly tend to suffer, Hocking (1923) has elsewhere pointed out, is that when we think about religion we usually naturalize it, whereas religion is of a nature such as resists being naturalized. Worship does indeed promote useful social ends. Its function, however, is not exclusively utilitarian. It demands a metaphysical object. To leave it with merely psychological attitudes or social tasks would be "illicitly to naturalize it."

Ackerman (1922) tells us that "religion not only subscribes to and sanctions the best morality, but moral character itself is religion objectified and realized." Antipodal hereto is the position represented by Stavenhagen's insistence on the total disparateness of ethical and religious values. That which should be distinguished and denoted by the term "sin," for example, is, he argues, in no wise the concern of ethics, even in the widest sense of this discipline (cf. Stavenhagen, 1925). Sin signifies either lack of an absolute personal attitude or the possession of such an attitude in an inadequate measure, as regards either the depth or the range of the experience. One may sin only in respect to God, as absolute being. The doctrine is connected with a conception of religion which stresses the "numinous," "absolute mystery," "creature feeling, *"majesta tremenda"* and thus, in spite of differences which Stavenhagen points out, leans heavily upon Rudolph Otto (1923). This profound writer has likewise insisted upon the unique character of the category of "the holy." The following are, according to Otto, the salient features of religion: "awefulness," "inward shuddering," culminating in the higher religions in the experiences of the "holy"; "creature feeling" with the correlative experience of "overpoweringness"; "urgency" or "energy" as expressed, for example, in the ideas of the "wrath" of God and the mystic's reference to the "consuming flame" of the divine love; incomprehensibility, incommensurability with the world of everyday experience, with imagination and with conception; "fascination," the impulse to approach the divine, to commune with the divine, to possess and to be possessed by it, to be saved. The attainment called salvation, unlike morality and goodness, cannot be "understood" or satisfactorily described. To the secular mind and outlook it is unintelligible. Stavenhagen objected to Otto's impassable gulf between the numinous and the rational. Bennett (1926) urges the same point and seeks further to vindicate the essential unity of the spirit by healing the breach between the holy and moral. "Since the numinous evidently implies some constraint, however mysterious, upon the conduct of the natural man, it is so far moral." Moreover, "moral obligation contains an element of mystery which is of a piece with religious awe." As for religious intuition, it "lives the death of reason as reason lives the death of intuition"; it is "a node in an alternating process through which conceptual knowledge must pass, a point of concentration which it reaches only to leave behind." Martin (1924) has likewise recognized that religion represents something unique, irreducible to morality, philosophy, or art. Its quality is that of mystery—save only to a psychoanalyst! Its ideas are not to be regarded as factual descriptions but as symbols and expressions of inner unrest, of repressed emotions and wishes acquiring a characteristic form of release. Religion generally espouses the popularly approved morality. But there is nothing in its own nature to determine the direction it will go, and thus the question whether or not a revival of religion would be desirable depends upon the nature of the ideals to which it would probably attach itself.

Pratt (1920, cf. p. 196) assigns to anthropology the questions of origin whereas Mueller-Freienfels (1920) devotes practically all of the first of his two small volumes in the Goeshen series to the origin of religion. The second of these booklets deals with myths and cults. With the particular forms of these and with the specific influences that have been operative in individual cases, the psychologist indeed, as the author sees it, has no concern, but only the anthropologist and the historian. Yet the psychologist alone can speak authoritatively regarding the universal springs in which the particular phenomena have their ultimate source. He must determine what basic needs are met. In any case he is on the search for psychological laws in order that he may exhibit facts in their psychological necessity. Runze's scholarly and richly documented treatise likewise stresses the problem of origins. His treatment and conclusions are of the most catholic sort, recognizing, in a manner admirably exemplified in Leuba's *A Psychological Study of Religion,* that most theories have erred primarily in their denials and in their exclusiveness, and that a genuinely empirical outlook compels one to admit at the roots of religious beliefs and practices many influences of very diverse sorts.

Of the general treatises recently published that of Pratt (1920) is of outstanding value. Eclectic as to the methods of acquiring and of interpreting relevant facts, it throughout exhibits a clear consciousness of precisely what is being attempted and accomplished, and in the course of the well organized volume practically all the major problems (save those of origins) receive at least passing discussion. Wunderle's introduction (1922) is interesting as coming from a Catholic author whose thought is based on that of St. Augustine. Among the British publications we call attention to Selbie's useful handbook (1924), obviously reflecting the influences of Pratt's *The Religious Consciousness* but in critical places rather seriously lacking in clear definition and scientific analysis; and to a somewhat more original introduction in which the author, R. H. Thouless (1923), utilizes a moderate psychoanalytic psychology. Much more extreme, and decidedly less convincing, is the book by E. D. Martin (1924).

It is remarkable how many efforts have been made to show in what ways the findings of psychology may be put to the service of religion. The Dean of Chester's discussion of "Coué and His Gospel of Health" is only one among the many publications that continue the early writings of Worcester and McComb on the relation of religion to medicine and to health. We would mention especially the books by Pym (1922, 1925) and Brooks (1923). Writing in a similar vein Barry (1923) has advanced the thesis that belief in God is a psychological necessity if the mind is to be completely unified. Very often it is pointed out that recent advances in psychology "have put new instruments in the hands of all those who seek to influence the minds and hearts of men" and that "no pastor of Christ's flock should consider himself adequately equipped for the work until he has gained some real acquaintance with the more important developments of modern psychology" (See Hardman, 1925, p. 25). The view is shared by the other contributors to the cooperative volume.

No less common, however, is the caution that the psychology of religion may be to religion a very dangerous ally. Much attention has therefore been paid to elucidating the limitations of any psychological approach. To cull more or less at random: Barry (1923) insists that psychology, as a science, is limited to a discovery of *how* things happen, leaving the question regarding the *why* to philosophy and theology; that origin must not be identified with value or be substituted for it; that a dismissal of the Object of religion on the ground of its psychological and social origin is as though modern science were declared illusory because of its source in magic and superstitions. He even ventures the assertion that the personality of God— indeed, "something very much like Christian Theism"—is the only basis upon which one can render psychological findings explicable; that "unless the Christian faith is true, psycho-therapy," for example, "itself collapses." Northridge (1924) reconciles psychological truths and their practical value with religious doctrines by distinguishing between the *immediate* and the *ultimate* causes of religious experience; moreover, natural laws "have themselves to be explained" and "in themselves require agencies to use them and cannot be identified with these agencies." Matthews (See Hardman, 1925) adduces the probable shortcomings of introspection in general; the limited nature, not of the *range* of the phenomena studied by psychology, but of the *questions raised about* these phenomena; and the restriction of science to description as distinct from explanation. Similar views impel Price (1924) to the conclusion that the psychology of religion can neither prove nor disprove any religious interpretation of life and that it therefore requires supplementation by philosophy and theology. Referring to the alleged contention of Leuba that the psychology of religion disposes of transcendental causes and to the antipodal theses of Pratt and of Wright, he maintains that this science can take note only of the human, psychical aspect of the experience process, and that any activity on the part of God could by the very nature of its inquiry not come within its purview. Hudson (1923), likewise misunderstanding Leuba, breaks a lance with him over the same issue. He insists that laws of nature are but descriptions, after observation of the facts, of how things happen and that they therefore explain nothing; they merely describe and dissect the mechanism of experience—they cannot decide as to ultimate origin or validity. Touching the thesis that God, immortality, the idea of a Savior, etc., are but "imaginary projections" he retorts by asking how the proponent of such a view rules out the possibility that his own opinion of religion is but a projection of his own weakness. Hudson takes his stand with those theologians who declare that religious experience does not contain its own sufficient evidence but that if it is "to be ascribed confidently to the God in whom Christians believe it must correspond in nature, significance and results with what on other grounds the Church teaches and believes about the character of God and his dealings with men." These other grounds are primarily historical, and the author admits that if they were undermined he would feel compelled to admit the possibility that his "own spiritual experience was simply the creation of his own mind strengthened through herd instinct, and so on, by the (equally deluded) religion of other people." Rose (1924) is of the opinion that Leuba expected more from the psychology of religion than "simply an ordering of the bare facts considered from the abstract point of view inherent in all science" and that when he met, as one must in such a search, with disappointment, he assumed the quest for God to be ended. Rose then argues for the necessity of admitting transcendental causes.

Staehlin (1921) seems at first blush to oppose those who contend that the psychology of religion is not concerned with the question of the truth of religion. What he really comes to say, however, is that psychology must describe and analyze the way in which the believer *experiences* the truth-*claim* of his religion. On the other hand, he holds that this claim is not the essential feature of religious experience. Religion, for him, is life, and life lays no further claim than that of being real and of being life.

Sheldon (1921) deals succinctly and independently with many of these contentions when he argues to negative answers to the following five questions: (1) "Does psychology cover so large a province as to leave no truly distinctive field or function to philosophy?" (2) "Is there good historic warrant for defining religion as the consciousness of social values, or as the recognition and pursuit of social values, thus leaving out of the definition all explicit reference to a felt relationship to a Higher Power?" (3) "Have arguments for the existence of God so small a measure of cogency as is assumed by some exponents of the psychology of religion?" (4) "Do psychological data involve any proper occasion or demand to negate the conception of positive revelation?" (5) "Is there reason for believing that a religion can be made to work successfully which ignores the idea of God and stresses simply a human striving for the good of society on an earthly theatre?"

Within psychology there have been strong tendencies to reject the distinctively psychic, or to think of the mind as ruled wholly by the body or as dominated by sexual passion, or to consider it a machine. Where has this left religion? The preponderance of opinion as represented by the publications of the past five or six years would seem to converge in the direction of Stratton's reply (1923) that "psychology leaves religion living, with new means for its great work and with fresh confidence in the naturalness and the need of the religious life. It is of help in pointing out religion's place and function, distinguishing it from art, science, and social (including political) reorganization."

Concerning the present status of the psychology of religion the present writer has written elsewhere (Schaub, 1922). A recent account of the history and the methodology of the science with particular reference to the developments in Germany has been furnished by Koepp (1920). Two papers relating to the history of the science and the work done in America have recently been published by the writer of this survey (Schaub, 1924).

A Critical Survey of the
Psychology of Religion

P. Hopkins

F EW OF MY READERS CAN HAVE ANY IDEA HOW LARGE IS THE NUMBER OF BOOKS
and papers which have been written to explain religious phenomena
from a psychological viewpoint. Since the number of studies, which began
with a trickle, has now become a flood, no one can claim to have read all
even of those produced in late years; and readers must forgive if in these
pages the amount of space given to critical synopses will not justly represent
the relative merits of the studies mentioned or omitted. The intention has
been to review recent books in more detail, generally speaking, than classic
works with which the reader is presumably already familiar.

Since some orderly arrangement of the material is better than presentation
by mere chronological sequence, I will divide my writers into half-a-dozen
broad schools of thought. A score of such schools might be mentioned; but
I will crowd them into the rational-naturalistic, economic-sociological,
anthropological, classic-psychological, libidinal, and eclectic groups.

RATIONAL-NATURALISTIC

In a brief article written primarily for contemporary psychologists, we
shall have to dismiss with brief mention the earlier and the more purely
philosophical writers. Among such I place the great classifiers of religion like
Hegel, Wutke, Caird, Whitney, Kueness, Jastrow, Jr., and Tiele. Nor can
more attention be spared for Herder, Carlyle, Renan, and (modernly) Dean
Inge and like theologians, nor for the old-time rational deists such as Vol-
taire and Thomas Paine.

With N. Bishop Harman's *Science and Religion* (1935), we come, however, to a book both more recent than any of the preceding, and with more
psychological coloring. Following in the steps of Thomas Browne, Mr. Harman attempts to answer the question (put to him by a student): How can
a man of science be also a man of religious faith? Knowledge of the difficulties, scrupulous fairness to the position of his opponents, and an attractive
style mark his reply.

His arguments are chiefly the philosophic ones—from the orderliness of
the world he infers purpose behind it; from its mechanism, design; from the
existence of personalities within it, that it is itself ultimately personal; from
the wide prevalence of beliefs, the likelihood that they are founded on

From "A Critical Survey of the Psychology of Religion," *Character and Personality,* 6 (1937),
16-35. Used by permission of Duke University Press.

facts; from the indestructibility of energy, the indestructibility of life; from the fact that "belief has been and is the mark of some of the most virile people of the earth," that belief is the attitude which goes naturally with mental virility; etc. Cases where prayer is not answered or miracles no longer performed, Dr. Harman excuses on the ground that we may not have met conditions which he explains. But the man is too honest to plead his cause from cases where prayer seems to have brought results, without explaining to us first how the psychological effects induced by our prayerful attitude may not have been the true causes. God's permitting of all the pain that exists in the world is the act of a father who brings up his children on Spartan lines—a statement on which modern psychiatrists may ponder quizzically.

Naturalistic interpretations may be said to date back to 1825, when we learn from Brillat-Savarin's *Physiology of Taste* (1826) that a certain *penchant* towards ecstatic states is easily explained by the effect which the change of position and temperature must produce on the brain; and this is another instance of the influence of the physical over the moral.

In my analysis of the above experience I . . . arrived at the belief that the exaltation of the *Orientals* was in part due to the fact that, being of the Mohammedan faith, they always keep their heads warmly covered; and that it was in order to obtain the contrary effect that those who made laws for our monks invariably impressed on them the necessity of having a part of their persons shaven and uncovered.

Methodologically a grade more important than such speculations was Sir Francis Galton's application of objective methods to the study of prayer. Comparing divines with other professional men, he found them less healthy. In persons of unusually great piety, he found sexual disorganization to be frequent. His work has recently been dealt with by E. L. Talbert (1933) in a paper in *Scientific Monographs* "On Francis Galton's Contribution to the Science of Religion."

In some cases, the natural explanation of the phenomena is to be found quite simply in the use of a drug. V. Petrullo, in *The Diabolic Root* (1934), studies the origin of a new religion called Peyotism, which has come into being since 1880 among the Delaware Indians. To escape from the sense of racial humiliation they took to eating an intoxicating cactus known as peyote; this gave rise to revelations; a ritual has sprung up; and government opposition has not prevented the spread of the cult even to the Canadian border. The individual and social significance of the whole train of events is dwelt on by Petrullo.

The next development of religio-explanatory rationalization was the emphasis on animism. Of this, the chief representatives were Tylor and Spencer, both of whom in the early seventies credited primitive man with working out a theory of souls logically from his experiences of dreams, shadows and death. Following Tylor, J. G. Frazer (1915), in his *Golden Bough,* tended to apply deductively to early man such principles as association and logical inference.

Meanwhile, from time to time, the latter half of the last century witnessed a vogue for an astronomical hypothesis about religion. According to this, the essential myths were symbolical allusions to the sun, planets, stars, and seasons. Such views are held by Dupoi's *L'Origine de tous les cultes* and G. W. Cox's and F. M. Müller's books.

Resembling somewhat the above were vegetational explanations. In the view of J. G. Frazer in the *Golden Bough,* and more especially in *Adonis, Attis, Osiris, Worship of Nature* and the *Myth of the Origin of Fire,* a symbolic account of the seasonal growth of vegetation underlay most myths.

SOCIOLOGICAL

Those who offer us an explanation of religions in sociological terms fall into two groups, according to whether they lay the particular stress on the economic factor or not. Those who do so are as a group less dispassionate in their approach than any but the very theologically biased. They are apt to be moved by a desire to prove that great betterments of human affairs would follow the adoption of some economic reform. The best-known essays of this type have been those of Communist and Socialist propagandists.

Karl Marx, in *Das Kapital,* maintained that the rise of creeds could be accounted for pretty adequately on the basis of the class struggle and the mutual advantages of an alliance between vested privilege and the ecclesiastical hierarchy. For the extreme form in which his doctrine of economic determinism has been promulgated by zealous followers, his collaborator, Engels, confessed in a letter to J. Bloch in 1890, that "Marx and I are ourselves partly to blame. We had to emphasize this main principle in opposition to our adversaries, who denied it, and we had not always the time . . . to allow the other elements involved in the interaction to come into their rights." Marx's thesis was amplified by Kautsky and notably by Lenin.

In 1917 the argument was taken by Mr. Upton Sinclair in his *Profits of Religion,* of which a new and English edition was published in 1936. It was a very thoroughgoing exposé of the part which mercenary considerations have played, and continue to play, in the policy of the great religious establishments of the world, and particularly of Christendom. He shows that churches tend to become great landlords on their own accounts, and to depart on other grounds also from the principles of their generally idealistic founders, in a way to favor the conservative outlook of wealthy benefactors. Psychologists will be somewhat interested in the accounts given in this book of the practical understanding of crowd management, and of the arts of quackery shown by Mormonism, Holy-Rollerism, Koreshanity, Mazdazan, Christian Science, New Thought, and their ilk. The book concludes with some speculations on what will need to be embodied in any religion which in the future replaces those which at present cater to man's longing for a cosmic outlook more friendly and "human" than science alone can give.

A similar theme is the basis of Mr. V. F. Calverton's *The Passing of the Gods* (1935). This writer regards man as more rational than is probably the case. So he attributes man's religiousness in the first place to an illusion that power was so gained over material phenomena. But science, Calverton continues, has undermined this basis by replacing this illusory power with real power. Yet, despite its absurdities, religion has till now held its place, and it has served certain interests. Thus we see the operation of what Mr. Calverton terms "cultural compulsives."

While Mr. J. F. Hecker's *Religion and a Changing Civilization* (1936) resembles the foregoing volumes in its concerns with economics, it lacks their hostility to institutionalized beliefs.

Three characteristics stand out very pleasantly as I put down this booklet. One is its fairness to the various beliefs described, which seems to come from a singleness of conscious desire to state the facts truly. A second makes this the more notable, for the author is much more interested in one especial question than in others, namely, in the stand of each sect upon economic issues. A third is the impression received that he could easily have made this a much larger work, had he not for some reason chosen to summarize his knowledge simply and briefly.

At the end of his presentation of the facts, he leaves it to the reader's own interpretation of them whether religion is so innate in man that it will persist through all future forms of society, or whether, as a mere product of circumstances, it will succumb to such dangers to it as Soviet Communism. He makes it very clear that the Bolsheviks *had* to fight the Russian Church.

The concern of this book is rather with religion as a generality, than with its specific forms—what it means to its practitioners, how it functions, what forces today challenge it, and what is to be its future.

Meanwhile, other non-economic, yet still sociological, writers on the psychology of religion were appearing. So great is the importance of our topic of the first two especially that the names must be familiar to all of us— Starbuck (1903), Ames (1910), King (1910), and LeBon (1913).

In 1915 appeared Emile Durkheim's *The Elementary Forms of Religious Life* (1915), in which he denied that the savage could distinguish natural from supernatural, placed immense importance on the division in savage interests between sacred and profane, identified early religion with totemism and the totemic principle with *mana,* and held that this and its thrill originated in crowd psychology.

From 1916 to 1919 Trotter (1916) produced some biosociological speculations on religion. His psychology is based upon the supposition of an "*instinct* of the herd." To this he attributed the varied types of mass action that had been described contemptously in popular language by LeBon, which had become so observable during the World War. Trotter here employed the word "instinct" in a sense which had merited the criticism of more meticulous psychologists. He failed to define precisely what he intended his term to cover. Secondly, he obviously included in it a great variety of responses which clearly are not given at birth at all, but are somewhat remotely derived by conditioning upon the more original responses.

Concluding the list of writers in whom the sociological approach is paramount, I will speak of Professor Margaret Murray. In her *The Witch Cult in Western Europe* (1921) and in *The God of the Witches* (1933), she maintains a position opposed to that of the psycho-analysts, and to those who stress the creation of demoniac figures as incarnations of repressed inner temptations.

Her thesis is that Christianity drove underground but never quite uprooted certain ancient pagan religious cults. (We have confirmations of this detail, by the way, in Lord Raglan's work on *The Hero* [1936]). An adjunct of such cults was service by priestesses. The so-called witches were, according to Professor Murray, simply these priestesses of a surviving paganism. It should be noted, however, that Dr. Ernest Jones had shown that witchcraft, if not created, was very amazingly and deliberately multiplied by the medieval church.

ANTHROPOLOGICAL

The chapter of the distinctly anthropological interpretation of religions may be said to open in 1891, with Codrington's *The Melanesians*. He was followed by Tylor, whom I have already mentioned, and J. G. Frazer then began his famous series, *The Golden Bough*. As late as 1934 six anthropological lectures of his were published under title of *The Fear of the Dead in Primitive Religion,* dealing with the use of force and deception, the barricading of roads by water or fire, and the mutilation of dead bodies to protect the living from ghosts. In 1909 another contributor of great renown, Marett, appeared on the field with his *The Threshold of Religion*. His most notable contribution has been to trace the origin of religion to an earlier stage than that of a belief in indwelling spirits such as Tylor supposed. Primitive man starts rather with a vague attribution to objects which the Melanesians call *mana*—an investment of an uncanny energy or mysterious fluid. R. R. Marett's *Faith, Hope and Charity in Primitive Religions* was published in 1932. In the same and the following year he delivered the Gifford Lectures, which have since appeared as *Sacraments of Simple Folk*.

Brief mention should be made of the Swedish savant, Tor Andrae, for his studies of Islam. In 1918 he commenced producing his works upon Mohammed. Shortly he added *The Origins of Islam and of Christianity* and the much-commented-on *Mystikers Psykologi*. A translation has made his

Mohammed: The Man and His Faith available to English readers, who will find it grounded in extensive research into Arabian literature to bring out the ancient Arabian, Judaic, and Nestorian background of Islam, and additionally the character and religious personality of Mohammed.

The best descriptive account which has appeared of day-to-day life in a spiritualist community is contained in *The Drama of Life after Death,* by George Lawton (1932). "Theology," he says, "describes the world in terms which fit human needs and aspirations," and this is the keynote of spiritism, the effects of which upon the believers, as well as the adaptation of its doctrines and practices to their requirements, are well described. The volume is characterized by objectiveness, thoroughness, and psychological insight.

Lucien Levy-Bruhl has for years been the leading French authority on the primitive mind. Dealing with the beginnings of belief, he upset the naïve rationalistic views of Tylor and Spencer that early man first formulated the hypothesis of a double and then extended it—in some communities this idea is preceded by that of plural souls. In 1935 Mr. Alcan published his *La mythologie primitive* and *Le monde mythique des Australiens et des Papous,* a study of certain selected myths. Professor Levy-Bruhl's researches are available also to the English public through *Primitives and the Supernatural,* a translation by Lilian A. Clare. A vivid picture is here given of the primitive's irrational mental life, as he moves in a capricious world of omens, talismans, amulets, ancestral spirits, witchcraft, defilement, and purification.

J. D. Unwin (1934) created considerable controversy with his *Sex and Culture.* Its essential thesis is as follows. We find three grades of sexual opportunity: (A) prenuptial freedom, (B) infliction of irregular or occasional continence, and (C) insistence on complete prenuptial continence of women. We find culturally three grades of religious development: (a) Zoism, (b) manism, and (c) deism. Now, invariably in whatever land or climate (A) is accompanied by (a) and (a) by (A); similarly (B) and (b) always go together and so do (C) and (c). In 1935 Unwin resketched the views of his earlier work, in *Sex Regulations and Cultural Behaviour.*

One result of the discussion aroused by Unwin's book was a tripartite debate between him and Drs. J. C. Flugel and R. Money-Kyrle, printed in the *British Journal of Medical Psychology,* in 1935. Unwin gives credit to psychoanalysis for having originally suggested to him that civilization was a fruit of sexual abstinence. Flugel contends that Unwin's work is not a verification of Freud's real view, which means by sex something much broader than employment of the genital organs. Money-Kryle suggests that the "social energy" which Unwin attributes to abstinence may be a collateral effect of some such things as infantile trauma.

We must also place among those making an essentially anthropological approach the most recent work of Eric S. Waterhouse—*The Dawn of Religion.* For although he admits a distinction between true primitive man and the modern savage, he argues that we may learn a great deal about the former by cautious deductions from a study of the latter. Indeed, the intrusion of Freud into the anthropological field with his theory on totemism is resented hotly at a length of several pages, where parallel conjectures of Frazer, Spencer, Gillen, and Durkheim are dismissed politely in a few paragraphs.

Professor Waterhouse, however, proposes himself to invade the psychological field as the only way of getting further back into religious origins than anthropology or history can take us.

He wisely declines to regard specific religious instinct as basic, despite the universal extent of the phenomena and the fact that "no substitute has ever filled the same place, or satisfied the same need as religion, in the life of the race." That the ultimate roots of religion are grounded in our instincts is the more accurate statement.

Looking for the primal religious emotion, the author discusses but rejects fear because it has unsuitable connotations. Awe, which is compounded of fear, wonder, and admiration, better fits the case.

Apropos of Levy-Bruhl's conclusion of the non-rationality of primitive man, Professor Waterhouse draws attention to the dependence of thinking upon an adequate vocabulary; "thought breeds up to the word-supply." The language of savages is replete with concrete terms, but deficient in abstract ones.

Several factors are admitted as causal in determining or altering the form of beliefs. The fact that innate tendencies of the human mind are everywhere operative is not to be dismissed. Transfusion of cultural elements must be given a greater place than has been done in the past, although not so great as claimed for it by the Eliot-Smith school. Individual reformers sometimes effect drastic results, although only so much of their innovations is likely to survive as remains congenial to their followers—a point which is illustrated from some movements among the North American Indians. Finally, besides the human contribution to the development of religion, it is suggested there may be also a Divine One.

CLASSIC PSYCHOLOGICAL

What may be called the classical psychological interpretation of religion began in 1882, when Professor G. Stanley Hall had a paper in the *Princeton Review* on the "Moral and Religious Training of Children." In 1904 he published his work on *Adolescence* that contained material on the religious perturbations of young people, and he founded his journal of religious psychology and education. His *Jesus the Christ* is a study of Jesus' emotions and their effect upon His doctrines.

Meanwhile, E. Starbuck's *Psychology of Religion* (1899) extended the position contemporaneously taken by Professor William James, to make feeling an independent source of experience; it also employed the concept of subconsciousness. The work dealt especially with conversion and with religious growth.

In the same year Coe wrote in the *Psychological Review* on "A Study of the Dynamics of Personal Religion." His book on *The Spiritual Life* tried to understand religious defections and looked forward to efficiency in religion as a means of bringing in converts. It discussed prayer, revelation, and mystic states. His *Psychology of Religion* appeared in 1916.

In 1902 Professor William James produced his notable *Varieties of Religious Experience,* concerned particularly with the phenomena of conversion and providing interesting material from individual cases. His *The Will to Believe* treated religion from a volitional standpoint.

In 1908 James Pratt also launched into this field with a notable paper in the *Harvard Theological Review* on the "Psychology of Religion." His most important work, *Religious Consciousness,* appeared in 1920. G. B. Cutten (1908) meanwhile wrote his *Psychological Phenomena of Christianity.* In 1913 Professor J. Mark Baldwin wrote in *The Sociological Review* on "The Religious Interest."

E. S. Ames's first work (1910), *The Psychology of Religious Experience,* was conceived from the standpoint of functional psychology. Ames stressed will as paramount to ideas or feelings. He dealt with the growth of religion in the race, and in the individual, and its place in life today. This book he followed in 1925 by *The New Orthodoxy,* by an article in *The Monist* (Vol. XX) on the "Psychological Basis of Religion" and one in the *International Journal of Ethics* (Vol. XX) on "Religion and the Psychological Life."

Another early contributor who has maintained his output consistently has been Professor James Leuba. In 1905 he was writing on *The Psychological Origin of the Nature of Religion,* and in 1912 produced *A Psychological Study of Religion,* while the *American Journal of Psychology* ran an article by him on "The Psychology of Religious Phenomena." His *Belief in God and Immortality* (1916) told the results of a questionnaire on the subject of conversion. In *A Psychological Study of Religion* (1912) he gave the results of a questionnaire. This ascertained that American men of science and college students tended more towards skepticism in proportion as they were eminent or mature. The greatest disbelief was as to the existence of God, less as to immortality. Psychologists were the most skeptical group, biologists next, and so on towards the chemists, physicists, and astronomers at the other end of the scale, the most believing. Professor Leuba inclines to dispose of all religious phenomena as due to suggestibility; this was the tenor of his *Psychology of Religious Mysticism* (1925).

In 1934 Kegan Paul published Leuba's *God or Man.* He here maintains that man has at great expenses of energy asked his gods to do what he can better do through science, and especially through psychological science. He credits religion for having promoted the cohesion of races and the consolida-

47

tion of states, although he is niggardly in acknowledging its further help in socializing individuals. But in any case, this service has been dearly bought by disservice and can be bettered by science now that it is turning its attention to the better handling of men.

In Part I of this work, religious methods are examined and compared to their disadvantage with those of science. In Part II, the origins of religion are inquired into, though without making any new experimental or theoretical contributions to this question, and the moralization of the gods, lagging behind rather than leading social progress, is described. In Part III, the religious mystic is admitted to be an experimenter who has hit on some useful mental therapies, but these are poor fumblings compared with what secular agencies do today. As cases in point, our clinics and juvenile courts are pointed to. There is discussion of such problems as intuition, inspiration, "the divine presence," and ecstasy, and science is declared to be not unaware of social idealism—although the book itself is not free from dogmatism under its admirable clarity.

Professor Morris Jastrow appeared quite early in this field in a *Study of Religion,* in which, as with Leuba, suggestion was invoked as chief explanatory mechanism. His *Psychology of Conviction* appeared in 1918, and has been followed by other works. He is, in fact, a highly prolific writer, aiming at a rather popular public, although he has a heavy, difficult style. His effort is continually towards exposing the mechanisms behind what he considers impostures; and these include not only all religions, but some of the new movements in psychology itself.

True to this description is a new book from this writer, his *Wish and Wisdom; Episodes in the Vagaries of Belief* (1935). A number of temptations towards error are here treated *seriatim,* each forming a division of the book—credulity, the thrill of marvel, transcendence, prepossession, cults and vagaries, and rationalization. Under head of each of these is given illustrative material which is apt and striking.

Professor Robert H. Thouless also was formerly much interested in religion. Notably, he had a paper on "Religion and the Psychical Life" in the *International Journal of Ethics,* and wrote a book called *Introduction to the Psychology of Religion* in 1923. Leaning a good deal philosophically to the Church of England, his treatment is very sympathetic, and the reader is impressed by great maturity of tone. More recently Professor Thouless, also, in the *British Journal of Psychology* in 1935, described his inquiries into "the tendency to certainty in religious belief." He found that in this field subjects did not maintain the reserve found on most matters of opinion, but believed or disbelieved emphatically.

This brings us to the experimental method of approach—not always easy to apply in the present subject. Some of the experiments have had as their goal to determine the extent of superstitiousness in certain environments, of the effect thereon of particular college courses. Of this nature were the articles by H. K. Nixon on "Popular Answers to Some Psychological Questions" in the *American Journal of Psychology* in 1925, and by G. Graham on the work of H. E. Garrett and T. R. Fisher on "The Prevalence of Certain Popular Misconceptions" in the *Journal of Applied Psychology* in 1926. In the *American Psychological Review* (Vol. XXI), there appeared an article by T. Okabe on "An Experimental Study of Belief."

Many experiments, too, have been carried out on claimants to mediumship or telepathic or occult powers. An example of this type was "An Examination of Miss George Dennis, 'Psychic'," described by S. H. Britt, in the *Journal of Applied Psychology* in 1932. G. White Read's *An Enquiry into Spiritualism* is a broad discussion in popular style, but with copious references, both of the human disposition to believe, and of the most famous and some other cases of telepathic, clairvoyant, and spiritistic phenomena. A suspended judgement is preserved, inclining a little favorably towards the milder phenomena, but against the most extraordinary.

Still other investigations have been made into the factors influencing persons to believe or disbelieve, as where G. B. Vetter and M. Green tell about "Personality and Group Factors in the Making of Atheists" in the *Journal of Abnormal and Social Psychology* in 1932. In three hundred and fifty questionnaire replies members of the American Association of Atheists claim as chief causes wide reading, disgust at hypocrites, influence of a particular author, etc., while factors like death, war, and futility of prayer rank lower. But 36 per cent were oldest children. In 1930 Professor Spearman included a chapter on "Ghosts and the Projection of Visual Images" in his stimulating booklet *Creative Mind,* based on his experimentally reached neogenetic principles.

We now come to Dr. J. B. Rhine's *Extra-Sensory Perception* (1935). His experiments, because of their simplicity and elaborate mathematical treatment, have created a very great sensation. They consisted in letting students guess which of five well-known symbols would appear on cards, when these were turned up. Certain exceptional persons appeared to guess correctly with far greater frequency than the laws of chance accounted for. The work of Dr. Rhine has been duplicated by other experimenters, at least some of whom seem to verify his results. On the other hand, his mathematical treatment has been questioned. Depressant drugs appear to diminish the alleged clairvoyant abilities, while stimulants temporarily increase it.

Readers of *Character and Personality* will recall Dr. Rhine's article in 1935 on "Telepathy and Clairvoyance in the Normal and Trance States of a Medium." In experiments on Mrs. Garrett, her scores were above chance, with notable similarities between her normal and trance personalities.

A critique by R. R. Willoughby of extra-sensory perception appeared in the *Journal of Abnormal and Social Psychology* in 1935. Willoughby offers grounds for expostulating against "the enormous odds which Dr. Rhine alleges against a chance basis for the correspondences." And he "found no very firm assurance of random sampling, and a few passages suggest that if a good subject made a poor record, it was forthwith discovered that he was ill."

Several classic-psychological studies have been directed to particular problems or particular cults. A work orientated more especially towards helping those whose problem is religious education is the *Normative Psychology of Religion* by Henry Nelson Wieman and Regina Westcott-Wieman (1935). By normative they mean "fulfilling of function," and they give religion a definition, more suitable for ethics, of devotion to the "supremely worthful for all human living." The work seems to have been influenced by Professor Josiah Royce's *Philosophy of Loyalty.* Professor Wieman is himself a philosopher, and joint-author with Professor B. E. Meland of *American Philosophies of Religion*—an excellent compendium, though outside our present scope.

Some aspects of Hinduism were treated of by R. Russell under the title of "Die Psychologischen Grundschrift an der Yoga-Praxis" in *Beitrage zu Philosophie und Psychologie,* in 1928. The works on Christianity are numerous. I have mentioned G. B. Cutten's *Psychological Phenomena of Christianity* (1908). There is also P. L. Couchoud's *Le Mystere de Jesus,* containing chapters on such subjects as demoniac possession, revivals, faith cures, Christian Science, and miracles. *Psychological Aspects of Mormon Group Life* was the title of a very interesting little book by E. E. Erikson, who was familiar with this American cult from his boyhood. Christian Science has also received some attention, more especially through several biographies of its able but neurotic founder. About the best known is E. F. Dakin's *The Biography of a Virginal Mind.* A really scientific study of such material waits to be made.

LIBIDINAL

Another important school of the last half of the century was that which stressed *phallic* symbolism under religious emblems, practices, and beliefs. Thomas Inman led off with a work on *Symbolism Exposed and Explained.* This was followed by Major-General G. E. R. Furlong's *Rivers of Life.* Then came a contribution by Luther Gulick on "Sex and Religion" in the *Association Outlook,* in 1897-98. In 1901 Hylan's *Public Worship* and Murisier's *Maladies du sentiment religieux* were published. One of the most authoritative books of this series was Josiah Moses's *Pathological Aspects of Religion* (1906), now out of print and hard to obtain. Finally, as we shall show, the phallic element has been stressed in recent Freudian literature.

Psychoanalytic interpretations of religious phenomena commence with Freud's famous *Totem und Tabu,* in so far as this was an attempt to explain the facts of totemism as then known to anthropologists in the light of knowledge about the Oedipus complex as gleaned in the consulting room.

There are several enlightening references to religious matters in Freud's extensive clinical and literary output. He does not, however, devote a book to the topic until his declining years. This work, *The Future of an Illusion* (1928), is written in his most mature vein and graceful language, but as a scientific argument it is disappointing in its lack of conciseness and in its failure to penetrate far into the depths of religious sentiment.

Freud considers that the mass of humanity can accept civilization only when it is forced upon them. They are reconciled to doing this by the possibility which religion offers them of sublimating many primitive instincts which civilization represses.

Religion is, however, a structure built out of the life of fantasy having but little relation to reality. The accumulation of real knowledge about the universe is making it impossible for an ever increasing number of people to accept these fictions any longer.

One of Freud's followers to take up early the treatment of religious problems from a psychoanalytic approach was Theodor Reik. An article by him on "Dogma und Zwangsiden" appeared in *Imago* in 1921. His principal study of this character, *Das Ritual* (1931), was translated into English a few years ago. The *International Journal of Psycho-Analysis* has printed articles by him on "Mysticism and Occultism," "The Therapy of the Neuroses and Religion," "The Science of Religion," "Mythology," and "The Strange God and One's Own God." Recently he wrote a book, *Surprise and the Psycho-Analyst* (1936), to explain and justify the process whereby the psychoanalyst applies the knowledge he had gained from analyzing one individual unconscious mind to interpreting other minds. Especially does he show how it can be properly applied to such psychological processes as forgetting (here he gives many case-histories) and (as in his own earlier work) to ritual. Another German writer is Dr. E. Harms. The title of his work is *Die Struktur des Religiosen Menschen*.

Several of the psychoanalysts are not unfriendly to religion as an influence with sublimatory, stabilizing, or palliative possibilities for the neurotic, or as transforming his individual illness into a collective and more social type. None, I think, would accept it as ever a *fully* curative agent; and I know of only one who is a professing religionist; I here refer to the Swiss, Pfarrer Oskar Pfister. The fourth chapter of his *Some Application of Psycho-Analysis* is on "Psycho-Analysis and Philosophy," and the fifth deals with "Psycho-Analysis and Missionary Work."

France, a country which was slow in taking up Freud's methods, has naturally been behind in producing religious studies from that standpoint. But in 1934 an issue of the *Revue francaise de psychoanalyse* contained an article by Marie Bonaparte on "La pensée magique chez le primitif." Grounding herself on various magical practices and beliefs, mostly cited from Frazer, Princesse Marie then presents the psychoanalytic interpretation. She follows this with an evaluation of magic practically and culturally.

America also has made its contributions to our subject. Prolific, among its analytic writers, has been Mr. Theodore Schroeder, who has to his credit a long list of papers in periodicals and of short monographs. And if Positivism is not too remotely connected with religion, I might mention an article in the *American Journal of Psycho-Analysis* by P. Blanchard on "A Psychoanalytic Study of Auguste Comte."

The leading English psychoanalyst, Dr. Ernest Jones, has made some extremely valuable contributions on our topic. If we are interested in mere superstitions, his study of "The Symbolic Significance of Salt" will be found a masterly example of the scientific essay, a closely knit argument based on great erudition. It is contained in his *Essays in Applied Psycho-Analysis,* which include also an essay of like character on the "Impregnation of the Blessed Virgin through the Ear"; i.e., an examination of the medieval legend, which had its counterpart in so many other religions, that the immaculate Conception was effected aurally by the Holy Ghost. Later religious essays have included "Zur Analyse der Christliche Religion" and part of a symposium on Christianity.

Dr. Jones' chief excursion into the field of beliefs, however, comprised the second and fourth quarters of his work *On the Nightmare.* This was largely composed in 1909 and 1910, but completed and published three years ago. Its first and third parts, the ones which most correspond to the title, are interesting to us here, only because it is claimed that nightmares are psychological relatives of, or even gave rise to, incubi, succubi, vampires, werewolves, witches, and the devil. The author easily demonstrates the lack of correlation between true nightmares (Ephialtes) and such alleged physical causes as gastric distress, and proceeds to offer psychological explanations showing them as consequent upon revivification of incest phantasies and masochism. Religion, especially Christianity, is regarded as essentially an attempt to solve the problems raised by man's aggressiveness—particularly by the Oedipus complex.

The five special medieval beliefs mentioned partake of the above characteristics of nightmares and of Christianity, to which are added certain peculiar determinants. The vampire conception owes something to oral erotism of the sucking-stage and to necrophilia. The werewolf is more indebted to biting-stage oral erotism. Incubi and succubi are derived more purely from the same incest sources as the nightmare. The witch beliefs are an exteriorization of the sex conflicts of women. The devil, whose medieval form inherits the nature-elements and startlingness and physical appearance of Pan, the hoofs and tail of German forest sprites, the red beard and body odor of Thor, etc., represents alternating emulative and hostile wishes

52

respecting one's father. As the author is an authority on philology and folk-lore, as well as on psychoanalysis, his pages are crowded with facts to the point where one at times loses the thread of the argument.

Among the earlier English writers whose approach was analytic was Dr. R. M. Rigall. His *Religion and Psycho-Analysis,* in which he seeks to show belief as objectively baseless, appeared several years ago.

Professor J. C. Flugel, in his very readable *Psycho-analytic Study of the Family,* devotes the thirteenth chapter to "Family Influences in Religion." He there explains how the ideal images which an infant forms of his parents —all-good, all-wise, all-powerful, all-loving, and, indeed, all-perfect—are not annihilated when with increased experience he "finds out" his father and mother in their true human frailty. Instead, they split off from the reality, to lead an independent existence as the gods, angels, heroes, saints, goddesses, virgins, etc.

In 1926 appeared Moxon's *Freudian Essays in Religion and Science.*

Another English book of importance is Dr. Money-Kyrle's *The Meaning of Sacrifice.* The stress here is laid less than one would expect on the Oedipus complex, and need of compensation for it, but upon other psychoanalytic mechanisms. Meanwhile, a number of valuable papers have been appearing in the *International Journal of Psycho-Analysis,* published in London. Its second volume included one such on "The Science of Religion," and another which was by Dr. Owen Berkeley-Hill, on the "Religion, Philosophy and Character of the Hindus." Dr. Melitta Schmideberg, also a member of the London group, in recent years has been publishing some papers in the same journal, which are extremely brilliant. In addition to their psychological penetration, these bristle with an almost appalling collection of anthropological and folklore data.

Finally, I should mention Dr. David Forsyth's *Psychology and Religion* (1935). For, although he is not strictly a practicing psychoanalyst, he writes from the angle of that body of knowledge, and incidentally he shows himself very accurately informed in it.

This book is, however, essentially, although not in any unfair manner, polemical. To Dr. Forsyth religion is antiquated. As one science after another demarcated its field of real knowledge, religion had in humiliation to withdraw therefrom. The history of this conflict is traced briefly in the book, as is that of the pagan origins of many Christian beliefs. Psychology has now wrested from religion its last stronghold, that of the soul. With its potent new weapon, psychoanalysis, psychology can even explain how mankind came to make the ridiculous suppositions which religion puts forward.

A defender of religion will remind us that when we explain we do not necessarily explain away. Also, he may, if a subtle philosopher, be able to point out some ways of escape for a refined deism which our author has not completely closed. But Dr. Forsyth's lucid, well-organized attack is very devastating. The volume concludes with an attempt to find substitutes for the faiths and practices which have been destroyed.

ECLECTIC

I have now dealt with such books as appear to be easily classifiable according to some special school. There remain those whose interpretations are more eclectic. Among these are L. W. Grensted's *Psychology and God* (1930), T. H. Hughes's *The New Psychology and Religious Experience* (1933), and Ernest M. Ligon's *The Psychology of Christian Personality* (1935). This last is not, as one might infer, a scientific analysis of the religious personality. It is a very straightforward attempt by the author to utilize his knowledge of psychology towards substantiating a series of sermons upon the Beatitudes. There are also F. R. Barry's *Christianity and Psychology*, K. Marechal's psychological study of the mystics, and C. Miller's *The New Psychology and the Preacher*.

In 1930 appeared *Psychology's Defence of the Faith*, by David Yellowlees. It met, as might be expected from the title, with considerable acclaim from the religious press. But its intentions outran the author's capacity, for his acquaintance with contemporary psychology was gravely defective.

This was, indeed, one of several books which have appeared lately as deliberate attempts to bolster up faith by recourse to the newly discovered facts of psychology. Unfortunately, they are generally written by clergymen whose defective knowledge of our science lets them down at critical times.

One effort of this kind was Mr. F. C. Carter's *Psychology and Sacraments*. The author, an Anglican clergyman, is a thinker of ability and candor, and his attempt deserves sympathy. He is troubled by dissentions within the church about sacraments. He trusts to bridge this and at the same time restore to pastors their old-time function as healers through the truths psychology has revealed. Mr. Carter makes a brave effort to stomach all of them, even the psycho-analytical ones which considerable sex-phobia on his part will not quite allow.

The spiritual life is likened by Mr. Carter to an attempt to bring a barge up a canal. Self-help (suggestion, meditation) gets us a long way. But when we reach a lock in the canal, we can be raised to the next level only by outside help—the sacraments. Penance and accepting God's forgiveness can help many people who now waste the time of physicians.

Confirmation allows a priest to impart sex instruction, preferably by handing out White Cross League pamphlets. Matrimony should be "contracted under conditions . . . likely to stamp the unconscious with the recognition of the sacramental aspect." Holy Unction should be restored to its original function of healing the sick. The technique recommended has three steps: probing the patient's mind with questions, terminating the heritage

54

of his past by absolution or prayer, and re-education by affirmations or prayer with meditation.

The author of this book has read widely in both academic and analytic psychology, and is at once eclectic and ingenious in his endeavor to use them for his purposes. The professional psychologist will not, however, deem him to have succeeded altogether well.

Dr. Henry C. Link's *The Return to Religion* is, for a "popular" work, a rather good, commonsense plea for going to church on psychiatric grounds. It makes use of much case material. The author is director of the Psychological Service Center in New York City. As such, he dedicates his book to "the millions of grandparents" who gave their children more than we give ours, namely religion. Dr. Link states that religion is a great support to these people against psychogenic illnesses. He brings in a great many case-histories to support his contention. At times, his discussion is psychological, but one searches in vain for evidence of familiarity with any classical psychologists of the subject such as Ames, Thouless, and others, or the analytic treatments by Money-Kyrle, Jones, or Reik, or anthropological views of such as Marett's.

Good and brief digests are given of the theology of Jeans, Haldane, Thompson, and Eddington. However, when discussing the attitudes of scientists to religion, he does not ask himself whether their competence in their own fields entitles them to be heard also in metaphysical matters; moreover, he mentions only those men whose views have moved in the direction of religion. Even so, he confesses that the "new concepts of God . . . are not particularly inspiring ·to worship." The scope of the book includes also Ethical Culture. The social gospel movement within the church as a means of keeping it alive he believes to be doomed.

In conclusion, let me say that, despite the great number of works which have appeared on the subject, the treatment of religious phenomena by trained psychologists is a field which has been no more than fairly opened up. One needs only to subscribe to a newspaper in a position to include occasional descriptions of exotic religious festivals (e.g., the Pinang *Gazette,* S. S.) or read some good summary of contemporary theological controversy (I suggest Wieman's and Meland's *American Philosophies of Religion*), let alone the well-thumbed volumes of Frazer and the anthropological books and journals, to possess a rich mine of fresh material.

The Psychoanalytic Study of Religion

R. P. Casey

AMONG THE VARIOUS RAMIFICATIONS OF PSYCHOANALYTIC THEORY, A NOVEL approach to the study of religion has been by no means the least significant. With the emergence of Freud's thinking from the phase of loosely connected but consistent reflection on various aspects of mental disease to a broader view of the foundations of psychic life in the *Introductory Lectures,* the possibility was opened for the application of psychoanalysis to cultural phenomena, and in subsequent years both Freud and his disciples have divided their attention between the clinical and social fields. The recognition of this dual task, implicit in the variety of themes treated in even the early psychoanalytic literature, was explicit in the founding of two periodicals, *Die Internationale Zeitschrift für ärztliche Psychoanalyse* and *Imago,* of which the former was medical in scope, the latter designed for the discussion of literary and social problems.

In the psychoanalytic study of religion Freud himself was characteristically the pioneer. His opinions are scattered through a number of his writings, but appear most clearly in *Totem und Tabu, Die Zukunft einer Illusion, Zwangshandlungen und Religionsübung, Das Unbehagen in der Kultur,* and in a neglected little essay, *Ein religiöses Erlebnis.* All these works are classic in their way but do not exhaust Freud's contribution to the understanding of religion, for his studies of a more special and technical kind— e.g., *Massenpsychologie und Ich-Analyse, Das Ich und das Es,* his observations on the nature of anxiety in *Hemmung, Symptom und Angst* and elsewhere, and in the case studies, notably the analysis of little Hans and of the wolf-man—contain significant implications which have in part been exploited by his followers, in part await detailed application to religious phenomena.

Totem und Tabu was the first considerable attempt to apply psychoanalytic insight to social phenomena. It established the parallelism between savage ways of thought, feeling, and behavior and those of neurotics living in more advanced civilization but retreating before it to primitive and archaic techniques of life; and it showed the basis of the parallelism in the relatively small advance from infantile interests and fixations. Specifically the book deals with the psychology of tabu as one kind of precipitation of infantile terrors and inhibitions. The tabooed person or object is the screen on which is projected the original fear of authority and deprivation. The complement of such fear is hate or, in more attenuated form, reverence accompanied by

From "The Psychoanalytic Study of Religion," *The Journal of Abnormal and Social Psychology,* 33 (1938), 437-52. Used by permission of American Psychological Association.

an imperfectly veiled hostility. Every god has his devil. Following a lead of Robertson Smith's, Freud saw in certain totemic customs—where the totem animal is regarded as the tribe's mythical ancestor and is as a rule tabu to the hunter but on special occasions slaughtered and eaten—an indirect reflection of primitive family life. The primitive rights of the leader of the human horde, especially his rights over the women, proved irksome to the young males, who finally rebelled and killed their leader and ate him with a view to assimilating his strength and privileges. In the background alike of savage custom and of his unflattering reconstruction of the primitive home, Freud saw the formation and operation of the Oedipus complex, that sinister and dramatic tension between age and youth over the retention and usurpation of the basic goods of life. The religious means employed in this struggle by primitive man were consistent with the childlike stage of his mental development, where the make-believe is real and where play, the religious counterpart of which is cult, can change the world at will through the *Allmacht der Gedanken.*

In *Zwangshandlungen und Religionsübungen* Freud pursued this question of cultus further and pointed to the similarity between savage rites and obsessional behavior. This resemblance applied not only to the form of rites but also to the attitude of internal compulsion and blind obedience to their set form, the logic of which, though real, is unconscious and hence concealed. Such ceremonies are protective and power-creating devices for the control of forces not merely outside but also within the personality. The *Allmacht der Gedanken* must be maintained even against rivals of its own kind and the swing of the ambivalent pendulum concealed by a colorful show of distracting emotion.

Die Zukunft einer Illusion, Das Unbehagen in der Kultur, and *Ein religiöses Erlebnis* deal with problems of contemporary religion. The essential in these writings is the clear perception of the limited success with which man pursues the goal of happiness and adjustment to his environment. Religion is an illusion in the sense that it refuses to accept actual limitations and declines to react to them with that modest circumspection which the facts commend. A scientific colleague had written Freud that he could not escape an impression of wonderment and awe at the prospect of nature and its secrets, "ein ozeanisches Gefühl," a feeling as if adrift on a broad expanse of sea, where no perspective is final and only a sense of vastness and majesty prevails. Freud, tartly disclaiming any experience of this emotion, explains it as the survival of an infantile awe of the adult world, a by-product of the desire to retain in the universe a homely and domestic setting. In religion the forces of nature are personalized to make them familiar and, what is more important, to make them susceptible to familiar methods of influence and control. The universe is, therefore, defined, in general, in terms to which its particular manifestations do not correspond.

Among the ablest Freudian students of religion have been Jung, Pfister, Rank, Reik, Jones, Alexander, and, more recently, Erich Fromm; though again a distinction must be drawn between works dealing directly with the subject at hand and those which have an indirect but important bearing upon it.

Of all Freud's pupils Jung has probably evinced the deepest and most sustained interest in religion. Unfortunately much of his writing upon it dates from a period when he had abandoned Freudian principles and attempted to construct an eclectic philosophy and psychology, based partly on psychoanalysis and partly on considerations of a widely different kind. Briefly stated, Jung's thesis is this: in all religions certain focal points emerge which give the clue to man's conflicts and aspirations. Since religion is largely a spontaneous product, it may be regarded as a kind of *lingua franca* of human nature, so that man's conflicts and their resolution (when resolution is possible) can be stated and dealt with in its terms. The recurrence in many forms of certain functional deities, expiatory rites and, more basically, certain typical feelings and attitudes, points not only to the source from which religion is derived but also the direction from which human nature is moving and the areas to which it remains enduringly oriented. That similar patterns recur in many religions, indicating important uniformities in the varieties of religious experience, was a view entirely congenial to the Freudian school. In the form implied in Jung's early work, *Wandlungen und Symbole der Libido,* it represented an ingenious extension of Freud's theory of symbolism in dreams and waking phantasies. But the schematization of the surface phenomena of religion in a comprehensive theory of life has not proved acceptable to men whose noses were kept closer to the grindstone of clinical routine and whose views of religion as well as of other cultural phenomena were controlled by a more rigorous and ruthless attempt to analyze human experience in the concrete and exact pursuit of therapy.

Oskar Pfister was a contemporary of Jung's who was attracted to Freud's views and combined their enthusiastic popularization with the work of a busy Protestant pastor in Zurich. He wrote a general introduction to psychoanalysis as well as several essays on religious psychology, among them a study of St. Paul and an illuminating discussion of glossolalia based on observation of an actual case of speaking with tongues in a Swiss peasant girl. His principal service, however, was a prolonged study of religious persons who came to him for help and to whose problems he applied psychoanalytic insight and modified analytic treatment. His work, therefore, on religious education, and on the place of religion among the causes and cures of religious people's difficulties, possesses a peculiar value. Unlike the professional psychiatrist, he was in touch with many problems not brought to a doctor's office and with many persons not amenable to conventional observation and procedure.

A brilliant but fugitive meteor in the Freudian firmament was Otto Rank. Originally trained as a business man, he became associated with Freud and enjoyed for a time his close personal friendship and warm professional admiration. His great work, *Das Inzest-Motiv in Sage und Dichtung,* is full of pregnant suggestions for the understanding of unconscious motives in well-known myths and folk tales, and his pamphlet in collaboration with H. Sachs, *Psychoanalyse und die Geisteswissenschaften,* a contribution of first-rate methodological importance to the study of religious fantasy and tradition.

Th. Reik followed closely in Rank's footsteps but extended his investigation of religion over a much wider area. In a volume of essays collected under the title *Das Ritual* he examined a number of primitive survivals in the higher religions, explaining their genesis in the operation of well-known unconscious motives for which clinical experience had provided abundant proof and illustration. In *Der eigene und fremde Gott* he showed how the combined and confused attitudes of dependence and attraction and of antagonism and revolt—displayed toward the parents in infancy and early childhood, and in later life toward figures possessing parental or quasi-parental authority (called ambivalence in technical jargon)—are transferred to religion and displayed in various kinds of piety. In *Dogma und Zwangsidee* he pursued a suggestion of Freud's to the effect that a significant parallelism exists between the grim persistence with which obsessive ideas are held and advanced by neurotics, and the attitude of faith in dogma, independent of evidence or logic, which is characteristic of some religious personalities.

Alexander's main contribution to religious psychology has been a study of the Buddhist goal of Nirvana. This he sees as an attempt to plunge the individual by artificial means into a phase of extreme regression, stripping the personality not only of the encumbrance of existence but of actual experience, and returning to the irresponsible calm of the intra-uterine stage of development.

Among the younger Freudians Erich Fromm, who brought to psychoanalysis a professional training in sociology, has interpreted the evolution of religious thought as an interaction between social forces and the deeper unconscious responses in the individual. Pointing out correctly that the essence of psychoanalysis lies in its attempt to relate the individual to his social environment from its very earliest stages, he insists that social psychology must rest on an extension of the same principle to the life of groups. "Die Methode der Anwendung der Psychoanalyse auf Gruppen kann keine andere sein. Auch die gemeinsamen psychischen Haltungen der Angehörigen einer Gruppe sind nur zu verstehen auf den ihnen gemeinsamen Lebensschicksalen." The corollary to this general statement is that social institutions and movements of thought, will, or action, must like individuals be analyzed in close relation to their environment and in terms of those unconscious motives and patterns which clinical investigation has brought to light.

As an illustration of this method, Fromm has selected the development of speculation on the person of Christ. In his view the development of christological dogma was to a large degree conditioned by the reaction of the masses to the social forces by which their life was dominated. At the beginning of the Christian era the lower classes in Palestine were oppressed by an aristocratic and powerful middle class among their own people and by the suppression and intrusive control of the Roman Empire within their gates. They reacted to this situation either by sporadic revolts and attempts at independence or by the projection of their hopes and fears in eschatological schemes and messianic expectations, in both of which impotent hate against superior force and the desire to reverse the privileged role were vital components. In the early stages of Christianity the majority of believers were proletarian. The emphatic non-resistance, the promised rewards of the poor, and disillusionment of the rich in the kingdom of heaven reveal their attitude toward the present and their hopes for the future. On a deeper psychological level, however, those resentments and aspirations became entangled with infantile conflicts with parallel structures, with the result that the two combine in the fantasy of Jesus the crucified Savior and adopted Son of God. Through identification with him the hostility against society—on the infantile level, the father—and the inevitable guilt engendered by such hate can be indirectly and symbolically expressed and a psychological equilibrium maintained.

With the expansion of Christianity over the gentile world new classes of people with different social attitudes from those of the oppressed Palestinian peasant joined the church. The State was reconciled, and the religious community became a society of brethren with a hierarchy corresponding roughly to the civil authority outside. Under these new conditions the notions of the relations between Jesus and God the Father, still faithfully reflecting the unconscious popular apprehension of the relation of the individual to society, changed accordingly. The doctrine of eternal generation and of the identity of substance between the Father and Son expressed a sense of reconciliation and solidarity with the social order. The unconscious significance of the Crucifixion was also modified, permitting not only an escape through identification for the suffering masses, but also the expression of gladly accepted subordination to higher authority on the part of the contented middle population, as well as an outlet for the guilt occasioned by overdetermined aggression among the tyrannous upper classes.

It is unnecessary to follow Fromm in the expansion of his theory or to attempt detailed criticism of his sociological and historical premises. The value of his essay lies in the suggestive attempt to equate social with individual processes of development and to interpret religious movements in social contexts with the help of psychoanalytic insight into the unconscious motives of behavior. The difficulties in such a procedure are obvious, especially when we consider the increase of variable and indeterminable factors in the problem. This is, however, a difficulty besetting all sociological and historical work. In the long run and with due care to its application, the addition of psychoanalytic knowledge and experience to the study of social history may greatly assist its understanding.

In 1930 one number of *Imago,* devoted entirely to the psychology of religion, contained besides the essay of Fromm's just mentioned contributions by Müller-Braunschweig on some psychological characteristics of the belief in God, by Reik on Jewish prayer shawls and phylacteries, by G. Langer on phylacteries, by I. F. Grant Duff on the visions of Ste. Teresa, the Little Flower, by O. Marbeck on the feast of the Midinettes, and a review of recent literature by A. J. Storfer.

This brief and imperfect survey of psychoanalytic studies of religion will give some idea of the breadth and depth of Freudian interest in the subject. Though it is impossible here even to summarize the conclusions of individual authors on the topics they have discussed, it may be well to characterize the literature as a whole and to estimate gains made and defects exhibited in it. Three main points emerge:

(1) Granting the validity of psychoanalysis as a whole, religion obviously presents a rich field for the application of its principles. The spontaneous growth of much religion, the primitive character of its attitudes and emotions, its frequently successful defiance of reason as a controlling element in life, and its production of explanations and pictorial representations of cosmic sweep, all are symptomatic of an area in human life in which the deeper unconscious forces have free and powerful play.

(2) The study of religion by psychoanalysis has so far been highly successful in pointing out many of the ways in which unconscious impulses and patterns are operative in theology, piety and cult; yet in attacking historical problems it has often been handicapped by obvious ignorance of the facts or defective perspective. Where the psychology has been sound and its application ingenious, the history has frequently been not only secondhand but second-rate, and the results obtained have had an illustrative rather than a definitive importance. No one can be expert in all fields, but a peculiar run of ill luck has attended the effort to psychoanalyze history. Freud's *Totem und Tabu,* valuable from everything but a historical point of view, was based to a large extent on the lamentably vulnerable anthropology of Robertson Smith, who believed that all primitive tribes had a tendency to sacrifice and eat their grandfathers. Jones' papers on religious psychology, in spite of much valuable insight, contain conclusions which a fuller knowledge and deeper sympathy with the evidence would have precluded. Reik utilizes the Talmudic accusation that Mary had an affair with a Roman legionary to

prove that Epiphanius betrayed his faith in the tale by a *Fehlleistung* (which unfortunately does not bear scrutiny when read in the context), and that an allusion to the tale is found in the line of the medieval hymn *Dies Irae* which reads *et Mariam absolvisti,* which refers to the pardon of Mary Magdalene, but which Reik sees as a gesture of Jesus to his Mother in pardon for the sins of her youth.

(3) The third point is the failure of psychoanalysts to realize as yet the full scope of religion as the instrument of the manifold unconscious motives. Even Freud can discuss religion in *Die Zukunft einer Illusion* as if it consisted in the main of a single experience, *das ozeanische Gefühl,* and a single complex of attitudes, the survival of the ambivalent feelings toward the father. No psychoanalytic understanding of religion will be adequate that does not reckon with both the variety of religious experience and the variety of unconsciously interrelated activities, attitudes, and emotions which religion either controls or influences.

We may now pass to a more systematic consideration of the value of psychoanalysis for the study of religion. One of the main devices by which the unconscious acts upon consciousness is projection, in the operation of which the logical and evidential components of ideas and the imaginative reconstructions of reality are obscured or pushed into the background. The effect is clearest in the more extreme examples of neurotic obsessions and psychotic delusions, but it has been found to be present in much more commonplace and everyday mental activity. Wherever the element of conscious rational control is weak, the barriers are let down for projection—as in poetry, art, and religion.

The projective element in religious thought and imagination is easiest to grasp in the case of religions other than our own. In the exuberant mythology of primitive peoples it can be detected at once. Even in the higher religions with their impressive theological façades there is always a datum to reason about: a myth, a rule of piety, a cult, which is rationalized but which neither begins nor ends with reason. History shows that even the high gods with their solemn metaphysical associations enjoyed a romantic, boisterous and often savage youth. Psychologically this fact means that notions about the gods involved responses of the individual to certain classes of impressions and aspects of life into which romantic, boisterous and savage elements were projected from within. The gods are terrible because by projection man interprets danger in terms of wrath and punishment. Dependence on the regularity of nature is felt as reliance on *Someone,* and the grim inevitability of destiny is accepted as a mysterious *voluntas abscondita.* Where do these projections come from, and why do they intrude so insistently on the religious field?

The answer lies in the nature of the unconscious, which is a storehouse of bad experiments and outworn apparatus. Attitudes which are taken up in infancy and early childhood, feelings which arise spontaneously only to be frustrated in their expression or discouraged in their repetition do not evaporate into thin air. They persist in the unconscious and penetrate in imperfect disguise into the society of adult impulses. It is in this sense that Freud has described religion as a "social neurosis," for the projection of attitudes derived from the germane to an immature adjustment to life and to the projected environment of childhood plays so large a part in its composition. It is another matter whether many of these attitudes may have a secondary validity and offer a clue to the right apprehension of reality as a whole. Psychologically their nature and origin are transparent, their means of operation in religion familiar by comparison with other areas of experience where projection is also an important factor.

We may now inquire what is the nature of these projected impulses and how they are satisfied through religious expression. The most obvious is the demand for protection against danger, protection against bad luck, protection against the sense of loneliness and indifference in life and protection against the sense of guilt in all its manifold forms.

Most of the high gods are strong and, in the main, benevolent parental figures. This observation is so literally true that many religions regard themselves as a kind of family and the conception of the divine qualities develops broadly *pari passu* with the evolution of family life. The savage god of savage societies is a not unfair infantile picture of the savage father in his savage home: terrifying, incalculable to the young in his whims and rages, yet not without consideration for his dependents, exhibiting a rough but genuine affection, and exercising an authority which is sustaining through its very familiarity. In matriarchal societies the mother goddess plays a stronger but never completely masculine role. Even in highly complex deities like Isis in Apuleius' *Metamorphoses XI,* in whom male and female attributes are amalgamated, the underlying attitudes which were once appropriate to the father and mother respectively can be distinguished, and the divine figures themselves are parallel to those curiously confused fantasies of masculine mothers and feminine fathers which so frequently play a forceful role in the genesis of some types of neuroses.

But it is not only the high gods who offer protection and help. In polytheistic systems and in religions like Catholic Christianity and Mohammedanism, the pantheon or the subsidiary figures of saints and angels provide an extension of the family circle. The attitude of the individual to these secondary personalities again follows closely the analogy of early home life with its nurses, older brothers and sisters, and friends of the family. The indulgent mother intercedes for the child with its stern father; the benevolent uncle will secure extra privilege or a relaxation of parental regulations; or on occasion the elder brother and sister will offer quasi-parental comfort or assistance when preoccupation or disciplinary measures deprive the youngster of the family of his needed props and care. A similar psychological situation is created or rather preserved in fantasy and transposed to the universe when, for example, Catholics feel they are pursuing their quest hand in hand and shoulder to shoulder with God's saints.

This kind of protection, whether strictly parental, as in the case of the high gods, or fraternal and amicable, as with the secondary deities and guardian powers, strengthens resistance against many dangers. The protection demanded of the gods against the more obvious external dangers does not so much reckon concretely with the dangers as rely upon the rough and ready experience and logic of childhood that the family group offers the alternate and only reliable safeguard. The mother snatches the child from the threatening traffic, the father beats off the angry dog, the older brother will sometimes fight one's battles; and the family hearth, with its friendly, affectionate, quarrelsome and at times antagonistic figures, is in marked contrast with the world outside the door where one is alone with the elements or thrown with incalculable strangers. The early sense of domesticity is too valuable to give up, even though it is subject to exceptions. Thus the religious man makes a home of his universe and preserves many of his original activities in it, for which in return he creates in fantasy and defends with argument the appropriate objects.

External dangers, however, are not the only or always the most important which man must face. There comes a time—and that quite early—when the child becomes afraid not only of others but of himself. Though many factors in its genesis stand out clearly, the origin of this fear or sense of guilt is complex and difficult of satisfactory analysis. The earliest impressions of discipline contribute largely to it; different individuals appear to be very differently affected by the discovery that theirs is not a solipsistic universe but an environment of other wills and forces than one's own. Even an infant's own most intimate property is not left entirely to his own disposition, for he is forced by a startling series of demands and frustrations to behave like others, to bow to convention, to accept values from without, and to curb and conceal his impulses and passions. Experiences of this type tend to precipitate and contribute to the formation of a nucleus of responses called "conscience." Thus when new situations arise, the disciplined habits of the past operate automatically in moral judgments and behavior, while the emotions of fear, subservience and aggression which accompanied the genesis of this moral attitude linger in the background of its adult exercise. In consciousness the fear of conscience is not the same as the fear of consequences, but in the unconscious it can be a stark terror holding all the primitive qualities of its infantile setting. This fear, furthermore, is one originally associated not with impersonal consequences but with the active threats of real people. Reminiscences of these figures inhere in the constitution of the conscience, which may on the surface operate with impersonal and abstract values, but which unconsciously is controlled by desires and threats. These threats and desires appear very plainly in religious forms of morality where the parental authority is assumed by the gods and goddesses and moral sanctions interpreted voluntaristically in terms of obedience and punishment.

The problem of guilt and the fear of punishment from within are, however, not exhausted by the practical situations which place moral demands on the individual. Many men are conscious of a guilt they cannot easily explain and for which no obvious reason is at hand. The sense of sin and of imperfection in general, religious scruples and the like which appear in consciousness without relevant content, have to be explained by some theory or myth of original sin—i.e., sin committed by someone else to the consequences of which man is irrevocably committed—or by the view that actual sin is so great as to leave no room for legitimate repose. These transparent rationalizations give only a partial clue to the origin of the conflicts of which they are symptoms. The need to shift the blame while accepting the consequences, a need characteristic of such states of mind, is indicative of an unconscious recognition of division within the personality. Likewise the willingness to submit to punishment for sin never actually committed is expressive of that peculiar disposition to court and to accept the known penalty rather than to chance the threat of suspected danger. This procedure is a commonplace among children, who often voluntarily confess their peccadilloes and set their own punishment in order to avert a surprise attack from authority when discovered unaware.

The explanation of this anomaly is that the unconscious threat is for reasons only partially understood much greater than the conscious one. A man may even take his own life rather than risk the judgment of others. Voluntary penitential exercises are unconscious attempts to anticipate a severer penalty by the assumption of one more familiar and less terror-laden. Here again religion operates in an infantile or rather domestic manner: the god may be appeased—and not always by appeals to ethical considerations. A whiff of incense, a slaughtered sheep, the prayers of the righteous and favored, who are in turn motivated by the burning of a candle or the recitation of laudatory petitions—these will sometimes let the believer off, just as parallel divides in childhood succeeded in averting or distracting parental displeasure.

It is from this vantage point that the whole field of cultus must be viewed; and the significance of rites and ceremonies should be gauged less by the sophisticated explanations given them in the higher religions than by their simpler and more obvious implications. An educated Catholic may explain to an observer of the Mass that incense symbolizes the prayers of the faithful rising to the throne of God, but the savage is sure that his deity likes the smell just as he himself does. Furthermore there is an obvious gap, or at least an uncomfortable sense of discrepancy, between the paraphernalia and action of many rites and the explanations offered for them. The reason is not always to be sought in the evolution and gradual refinement of theology but in the fact that at bottom the rites symbolize unconscious, not conscious, patterns of fancy, the content of which is remote from that of the rationalized explanations. Just as the notion that incense symbolizes prayer has supervened upon the more forthright view that its odor is pleasing to the god and worshipper alike, so also the crude fact of smoke and smell have unconscious connotations which are highly relevant to the subliminal drama of the rite. Ritual, as Reik and others have shown, is parallel to the neurotic mechanisms of behavior as much as religious thought and fantasy are illustrative of projection. In technical language ritual is a sublimated compulsion; dogma and myth, sublimated obsessions.

This brief survey of the history and formulation of psychoanalytic views of religion suggests several considerations for its future development:

(1) There is a great need for new material of a kind more susceptible to experimental observation and control. Neither anthropology nor history is an ideal starting point for investigation. The minds of savages are difficult to penetrate even by the most skillful and sympathetic outsider, and the easy equation of their attitudes and fantasies with those of childhood is a radical over-simplification of the problem. Historic characters even more than living savages are elusive subjects for analysis, since their interpretation depends largely on analogies which must be pressed beyond the available evidence. Hence the material tends to be forced into rigid categories of symbolism or dissipated in plausible conjectures about its motivation and significance.

The source of reliable knowledge, however, is at our doors, and studies are urgently needed which are based directly on contemporary clinical experience. It is a commonplace in analytic practice that religious personalities shift their ground under analysis. The cover for an aggressive impulse may serve as the vehicle of its release in religious as in other types of material. Changing religious attitudes and varying emphasis on specific doctrines may reveal the relaxation of tension within complexes, while mythological details indicate transformations or resolution of obsessions. Although all this is accepted and regularly taken in the normal therapeutic stride, its careful collation and study would provide a solid and secure basis for understanding the place of religion in the dynamics of human life.

(2) A point to which special attention should be directed is the problem of guilt. This pervasive but elusive factor in personality is brought more boldly into the open by religion than by any other substitutive device. Clinical studies of religious guilt, both in its conventional or cultic forms and in its more spontaneous expressions, could shed much light on problems of ambivalence and on the interrelation of sado-masochistic tendencies and their constitutive importance for some kinds of religion. The way to this

kind of investigation has been pointed out by Freud in *Hemmung, Symptom und Angst.* An essential presupposition to it, however, is the realization that religion undergoes many transformations in the process of its assimilation by individuals and that a view of the total individual personality, as well as a perception of the emotional flexibility and manifold emotional potentialities of different religious systems, is indispensable.

(3) The question should also be raised whether any correlation can be established between different types of neuroses and psychoses and the kinds of religious experience and behavior exhibited in them. It is probable on general grounds that schizophrenics, manic depressives and the feeble-minded find religion of varied and characteristic service to their needs, but the extent of this differentiation is unknown and its implications for the understanding of religion unexplored.

(4) An important problem both in theory and in practice is the extent to which religion is the handmaid of symptoms and in what specific ways it may become a sublimation. This is so individual and practical a question that fixed rules would no doubt be hard to formulate, but experience might prove an unexpectedly efficient guide. The psychological evaluation of religion in terms of evidence rather than of hypothesis would represent a substantial gain.

It is commonly assumed that the psychoanalytic way of looking at religion must be an outsider's way, and that the implications of discoveries which ally religion to the abnormalities of mental life and action can only prove it to be a disease of which humanity should be aware and from which it should seek a speedy recovery. This view is not without its adherents and a certain justification. Freud maintains it, describing religion as *ein stück Neurose* in the evolution of humanity which in its maturity it must discard. *Die Welt ist keine Kinderstube,* he writes, and grown men cannot afford in the long run to speak, think and act as children. Even within the limits of psychoanalytic theory, however, this view cannot be completely justified. The unconscious impulses and patterns which are revealed by analysis as immanent forces in religion are generally pervasive in human nature and can be neither completely eradicated nor controlled. Like Kant's categories they are to some extent prismatic factors in knowledge and in the determination of value, imposing the terms on which values are perceived and formulated.

All this is especially true in ultimate questions which are the real sphere of religion—questions for which in large part the evidence is insufficient to support an assured answer, so that one is turned adrift on conviction, i.e., emotionally charged hypotheses. As humanity has advanced, the problems of ignorance have become fewer but bigger. In areas where concrete knowledge is possible and the application of logic to evidence can be made, projective thinking should be controlled and behavior conformed to the dictates of reason and common sense. But many of religion's problems are not of this order and have become problems only because they have been posed from within in forms not modeled by the adult's outside world. Psychological analysis of the dialectic of religion, referring us to infancy and childhood, acquaints us with impulses which are often corrected or discarded in the process of adjustment to material requirements. The question, however, remains as to whether their implications are not as profound as their roots are deep.

The Psychological Understanding of Religion

Seward Hiltner

IF WE HAD WISHED, A HUNDRED YEARS AGO, TO FIND A SOURCE OF WHAT WE should now call insights into the psychological understanding of religion, we should have been led into many strange paths and blind alleys.

We might have tried the academically respectable source usually known as "mental philosophy." There, amid the abstract entities of intellect, will, and emotion we should have found ourselves floating far from anything which in our experience was related to religion in the lives of people.

Had we gone to the theologians and philosophers of religion—the philosophical theologians and the theological philosophers—we should have discovered a great to-do about monism and dualism, about spirit and matter. Since we should have had a religious interest anyhow, we should probably have adopted their prevailing idealism against the rising materialism and empiricism. But we should not have received much insight into the way religion actually functions in human life. Before we were aware of what was happening, our question would have shifted to the objective truth of religious beliefs and the validity of religious experience—instead of sticking with an understanding of what the experience is and means and how it comes about.

We might have learned more if we had gone to some of the less systematic

From "The Psychological Understanding of Religion," *Crozer Quarterly,* 24 (1947), 3-36. Used by permission.

thinkers, but more acute observers of individual people, such as Horace Bushnell or Ralph Waldo Emerson or Lyman Beecher. After all, they were preachers. As such they were so well convinced of both the truth and validity of religious experience that they could afford to take a few things for granted; hence they paid attention to some matters which the philosophers felt were too concrete to warrant their idealistic attention. If we had the good fortune to stumble on some of the works of Jonathan Edwards in which he did some rather acute dissections of personality, or to meet the preacher of the 1830's who said that he always assumed that the problem presented was not the real problem until it was proved otherwise—then we might have been closer to what we were seeking. But our findings would have proved so unsystematic that we should probably have got from them no more than some good leads.

We could, of course, have turned back into history with some profit. Perhaps first to the Roman Catholic and Anglican books on moral theology, on ascetical theology, and even to the penitentials. We should have found them full of insights into motivation. Our conviction that neither religious intensity nor breadth of religious perspective is an infallible sign of sound religion would have been reinforced. But we should have foundered, nevertheless, on rocks of formalism, of abstraction, and of preoccupation with punishment and blame. We should have seen abstract religious problems rather than real people experiencing religion.

Perhaps, if we had been godlike in our wisdom, we might have sought out some missionaries who were being forced to think through the meaning of their religion, through coming in contact with strange and foreign cultures and religions. Here on this continent we might well have marveled if we had read accounts by missionaries of the culture and religion of the Plains Indians, and then had contrasted those with accounts of the culture and religion of the Indians of the Southwest.[1] What was happening to the people of the Plains when they assumed the necessity of ecstatic experiences, the normality of visions and hallucinations after extended fasts, the partial relationship of alcoholic inebriety and religious ecstasy? In contrast, what was going on inside the people of the Southwest with their endless rituals, their cultivation of emotional plateaus, and their rejection of ecstasy? We might have had to think through the answers to these questions for ourselves; but we should certainly have been dealing with questions of the psychological understanding of religion.

Even if we had gone, a hundred years ago, to all of the available sources, our pickings would still have been very meagre. We should not so much have found the wrong answers as we should have been diverted into asking the wrong—from the psychological point of view—questions. In mental

[1] See Ruth Benedict (1934).

philosophy our questions would have been too abstract to touch real people. In philosophical theology we should have been led to feel that a non-metaphysical interest, or an interest with other than a metaphysical aim, was the same as an antimetaphysical interest; and we should simply have become theologians or philosophers. If we had gone to the farsighted preachers, we should have been a bit closer to psychological questions concerning people, but we should probably have been saddled with a narrow concept of and preoccupation with "normality," and possibly with a vulnerable moralism. With moral and ascetical theology we should have been led to feel that the important question always is: Is it right or wrong? How it operates would have assumed such minor and subsidiary significance as to deserve no more than passing mention. And even if we had followed the missionaries, our question would have become: How can we get these people to accept Christianity? We should have left behind questions as to the meaning of their own religion to people in other cultures.

We must face the fact, therefore, that the psychological understanding of religion, as any of us would conceive it today, is of relatively recent origin. I have sympathy with those among the theologians who find in the history of Christianity perception into important truths whose origin the modern refuses to acknowledge. I am also sympathetic to those who find, for example, in the writings of John Calvin deep flashes of what today we should call psychological insight into the way religion operates in human life. And yet these do not mean that Calvin or the others are interested, in the way we are, in the serious study of the psychological meaning and function of religion.

Credit must be given, in view of these facts, to the rise of natural science and of empiricism for those indispensable conditions without which study of the psychological understanding of religion would have been impossible. This is not to get ourselves enmeshed in the theological and philosophical issues centering around truth and objectivity. By being psychologists we cannot escape those issues. But, regardless of the stand we take in relation to them, we must see the study of the psychological understanding of religion as important. Within the empirical field, therefore, empiricism has won its point. The psychological understanding of religion is important. Just how important it is in relation to the philosophical and theological questions about religion is not itself a psychological question.

THE BEGINNINGS

During the latter part of the nineteenth century, and culminating in the twentieth, scientific method not only came into wide use but for the first time in history it seriously influenced human thought in general. It presented such vistas of possibility that the very meaning of "empirical" became different from what it had been before. Empiricism, as the philosophy giving exclusive exaltation to the empirical, became for the first time a non-Stoical possibility in history. This was the time when realism began to combat romanticism in literature, when naturalism got a toe hold on idealism in philosophy, when modernism began to fight fundamentalism and revivalism in theology, when impressionism battled neoclassicism in art—and when in various ways the empirical approach was set to solving the social and political and economic problems of society through such diverse means as the founding of sociology, the rise of Marxism, the growth of the social applications of Christian teaching, and the like. We know also how much all these and similar movements came into being as reactions against previous movements, and had therefore a pendulum character which could not permanently be sustained in their original motion. At any rate, it was in such a context that modern psychology arose, and in which the study of the psychological understanding of religion had its beginnings.

Wilhelm Wundt (1902) is usually considered the founder of "experimental psychology" and is therefore the father of modern psychology. For by taking psychology into the laboratory he freed it from being a handmaiden to purely idealistic or rationalistic philosophy, where it had been since the days of Thomas Aquinas and indeed of the Greek philosophers. It is not intended here to attempt any history of the rise of modern psychology in general. But we may recall that psychology developed largely according to the lead given by Wundt, in the attempt to apply the methods of the physical and biological sciences to mental phenomena. Much of the work along these lines may be evaluated as fruitful, even though not much of it is relevant to an understanding of personality psychology.

Even in Wundt himself, however, there were tendencies and interests broader than those of the laboratory. Wundt (1902a, 1916) wrote both on moral problems and on primitive social psychology. With the American material chiefly in the forefront of our thinking we may forget that it was in this country alone that laboratory methods were carried to extremes in psychology, and that in Great Britain and on the Continent broader questions were asked at all times. In France some social psychologists, notably Emile Durkheim (1915), were interested in the psychology of religious origins. These Continental workers were half empiricists, half rationalists, and what emerged from their work seems to us today to be largely speculative in character. They did not ask, for the most part, the questions which we should now consider to be the dynamic questions.

Before moving to America, we might do well to mention *The Golden Bough* and what it symbolizes (Frazer, 1915). Material had been piling up for a long time which would have made possible some study of comparative cultures, and indeed modern cultural anthropology got started before this book was published. But Frazer was the first to capture public imagination by setting forth the breadth and variety of the comparative cultural material. Potentially, cultural anthropology has as much significance for demonstrating and disclosing the operating dynamics of religion as does psychological study within our own culture. But because Frazer was not a firsthand observer, because his method was nonintegrative, and because it involved only the comparison of similarities and differences whose criterion was superficial rather than in terms of what any particular action or custom meant to the peoples themselves, it probably gave some bad leads to the psychological understanding of religion. But Frazer had performed a public relations function of real importance.

We have seen how, in Europe and Britain, the first modern study of religion from the psychological point of view was preoccupied with primitivity. In America the essential fact was similar—but primitivity of a sort was at our back door. Some of the American phenomena of revivalism, for instance, which could be seen with the naked eye, were similar to what the European academicians, with their more rigid code of what was and what was not a subject of respectable study, could find only through study in books. When William James (1902) gave his Gifford Lectures on *The Varieties of Religious Experience* in Edinburgh, I feel sure that, over and above his knowledge and charm and style, an astonishing thing to his hearers must have been the quality of firsthand contact which he seemed to have in relation to the data under discussion. Scotland certainly had unusual religious movements, but these were there set apart from a rather rigid ecclesiastical norm. Scotland, in other words, was not a frontier. America was. James got most of his case histories from books. But at that time only an American could have used case histories at all.

A more direct way to come at the point is to say that the psychological study of religion has generally applied itself to phenomena which have been prominent in the particular cultural pattern but which have begun to lose their hold. In Europe this meant a study of primitivity and of origins. In America it meant study of revivalism, of bizarre forms of mysticism, and of adolescent sudden conversion experiences. This was in line with the general trend toward reductionism in all the sciences of that time. Biblical criticism, for example, got away with Old Testament analysis before it could do so with New Testament study. Man's naturally strong suspicion that analysis of a thing changes and depreciates its meaning was augmented by the philosophical attempts to do just that. Small wonder if the psychologists of religion sought slightly safer ground by choosing for investigation those phenomena which did not clash openly with generally accepted *mores,* or with *mores* of the respectable group whose approval they sought.

In America, G. Stanley Hall, in connection with his studies on adolescence, published an article on religious conversion in adolescence as early as 1881. During the remaining years of the nineteenth century attention was devoted to the same subject in articles by other psychologists including

William H. Burnham, A. H. Daniels, and E. G. Lancaster. The observations were general, however, and of limited extent until the full-length work of Edwin D. Starbuck (1903).

His book is the first full-length treatise in the American tradition, and it is not unimportant that it was first published in London and only later in America. Its analysis of the phenomena of conversion threatened patterns which, while not dominant in America, were still prevalent here. In Britain such patterns, while not absent, had comparatively little "respectable" support; hence were not the same threat as in America. Starbuck associated conversions of the sudden type with adolescence, and he tended rather uncritically to view adolescence as a psychological fact requiring little or no social or cultural explanation. The important positive point which emerged from his work was that even the most bizarre-appearing religious behavior has causes and meanings which are susceptible to being traced. He qualified the point incorrectly by drawing a sharp line between religious and "abnormal" phenomena, refusing to concede a religious label to the latter. His main point stood nevertheless. It may also be noted that he was content to present his data and findings and to draw limited generalizations from them. He did not feel the necessity of going on to apologetics or polemics and asserting that therefore all religious phenomena were or were not true or good.

Despite the fact that Starbuck was the first to present an extended study of religion from the psychological point of view, William James was undoubtedly the most influential among the pioneers. Seen in the perspective of the present, at least the following were among the major contributions of James' work in the psychological understanding of religion. First, he created enthusiasm for and interest in the subject, a matter of no small importance. Second, he used empirical material, but put it in a framework which made it clear that psychology was not sufficient by itself. Third, he gave impetus to a new vantage point for evaluating religious beliefs not so much in terms of their truth as in terms of their operational significance in human life, i.e., whether they were "healthy" or not. Fourth, he turned attention to more contemporary empirical methods in studying religion, to observable phenomena, and not merely to documentary accounts of primitivity. Fifth, to some extent he applied his study even to those types of religious functions which were "fashionable," and not merely to those which were of the recent past. Sixth, he helped greatly to overcome the distrust of psychological study of religion as such by demonstrating that his own study had not made him lose interest in religion in a personal sense.

It is not easy to know how to assess the contribution of J. H. Leuba in the beginnings of this study in America. By the mid-nineties he was publishing articles on the psychology of religion, and he was partly responsible for the early concentration of interest in sudden conversion phenomena. He does not seem to have done firsthand observation; and, unlike James, his general attitude to religion has been anti rather than pro. Indeed, Leuba was the earliest and most obvious reductionist among the psychologists of religion. Because of his scholarship, his works had to be taken seriously. But no one liked them except those whose attitudes also demanded a dethronement of all gods. Since this was the clear, and eventually the stated, purpose of Leuba's work, it is doubtful how much he may be considered interested in a psychological *understanding* of religion. His chief contribution has been as a stimulator of more positive thinkers. [2]

E. S. Ames (1910), basically a philosopher rather than a psychologist, performed an important service by showing how influential sociological factors are in determining the form which psychological patterns shall take. But since his main interest was in empirical naturalism, he contributed toward the idea of reductionism which had become tied up in a special way with the "psychology of religion."

Irving King (1910), the first of the religious educators except George A. Coe to turn to the psychology of religion, attempted to use the new tool to discover how religion actually develops in people. He turned his attention to many aspects of religion, even to the significance for it of the emerging psychotherapeutic movement. His main contribution is in suggesting that the psychological study of religion has significance for Christian nurture.

The first British book in the field seems to have been that by G. M. Stratton (1911). This study was based on books, and was an attempt to build a psychology of religion through comparative book study of common and different elements in various religions. The elements compared were too isolated to yield data for a far-reaching psychological understanding of religion.

George A. Coe (1902, 1916) belongs very nearly at the head of the list of pioneers. The work of no one else but James has stood the test of time so well as that of Coe. Although his major book in this field was not published until 1916, he had published various articles before that, and from the beginning all his writings possessed a strong psychological orientation. Although Coe was a religious educator, and later permitted his interest in the psychology of religion to languish in favor of religious education, he was in many ways more of a psychologist in our modern sense than was any previous writer in the field. Despite his monumental work on psychology, William James was essentially a philosopher. So were Ames, Stratton, and Leuba. Starbuck was a psychologist, but in a sense we should now consider narrow. It is not strange, then, that Coe, with personality psychology at the forefront of his attention, and with fine scholarship in theology and religious education, should have written on the psychology of religion in a way which has stood up for thirty years.

[2] His best book is *Psychology of Religious Mysticism* (1925).

74

One additional pioneer must be mentioned, J. B. Pratt (1907, 1920). Although his full-length work in this field did not appear until 1920, he had published a previous book in 1907 and numerous articles in between. Pratt is rambling, discursive, chatty, intelligent, and an armchair worker. He knew the difference between psychology and theology, and made a real attempt to discuss only the questions to which psychology was relevant. But all his efforts were directed to essentially philosophic and theological questions, even though he discussed only those aspects of them to which psychology had a contribution to make. For these reasons Pratt has always been a favorite among philosophers and theologians, gaining more attention in a sense than he has rightfully deserved. He apparently failed to see the implications of the coming dynamic psychology; yet he mentions Freud, shows that he has read him though without comprehending the revolutionary character of Freud's work. One cannot but respect Pratt's good sense, scholarship, and genial insight; but he is a philosopher's psychologist and not a pastor's or a psychologist's.

IMITATORS OF THE PIONEERS

When pioneers have staked out large claims and put in the stakes in a certain way, it is natural that for years afterwards they will have imitators who try to stake claims in exactly the same way. The psychology of religion has been no exception.

G. B. Cutten (1908) collected a lot of data but treated them only popularly. Elmer T. Clark (1929) thirty years later redid Starbuck's study with substantially the same methods. A rash of works in the 1920's, when psychologistic thinking was popular, were generally mere imitations of the work of the pioneers in the psychology of religion. That of R. H. Thouless (1923) was the first general text in Great Britain. Others which have failed to make a distinctive mark were by W. B. Selbie (1924), Frank S. Hickman (1926), C. C. Josey (1927), J. C. Flower (1927) and F. L. Strickland (1924).

During the past year Paul E. Johnson (1945) has published a general volume, the first new text since the twenties. In its general outline, list of subjects considered, and in several other features, it must be classed as an imitator of the pioneers. In certain other respects, notably Johnson's belief that dynamic or therapeutic psychology has created new bases for the psychological understanding of religion, it belongs in a different group, and leads in the same direction as does this present article.

E. S. Conklin (1929) must, regretfully, be placed in the imitators' category. While more interested than most others in demonstrating the psychology of religion as a legitimate interest and branch of psychological study in general, and being himself a psychologist, his treatment is nevertheless lacking in any basic originality and is without the acuteness of some earlier works, like Coe's.

75

It is worth noting, while on the subject of the imitators, that almost the only way to have a piece of research or writing classified as "psychology of religion" for the past twenty-five years has been to put those words in the title. This is further borne out by a count I made a year or two ago of courses on the psychology of religion in theological schools. Nearly all the seminaries had one course invariably titled the psychology of religion or a rough approximation thereof; and almost no seminaries had additional courses in the field. This underscores the brilliance of the mark left by the pioneers upon the theological world, but it suggests further that the illumination apparently produced much blindness. Few followers thought seriously of altering the basic orientation. Thus, in an important sense, the field currently known as the "psychology of religion" has itself become an imitator. New work, new viewpoints, and new insights—of which there have been a number—have been called by other names, even though they belong clearly in the stream of tradition founded by James, Starbuck, Pratt, Leuba, Ames, and Coe.

THE PHILOSOPHICAL STREAM

If we glance over the list of persons who are pioneers in the study of the psychology of religion, we note that none made this field his major interest. Some were or became philosophers; others, religious educators; others, general psychologists. In no other field of theological study has such a situation occurred and there must be reasons. The obvious ones are these. No institution of learning has ever enabled a man to devote his full time to it. The recent resurgence of interest in theology has given its study such prestige in religious circles that the theological *mores* now include all religious analysis, even of a psychological nature, under the technical category of theology. Religious study has been under a cloud in scientific circles until recently, and psychologists who had an interest in religion wanted to make sure that they devoted only a part of their attention to religion in order to maintain their respectability.

There are, however, deeper reasons for the failure of the psychology of religion to develop as a proper field of theological study. Much in the early work was of searchlight quality. But it was analytic, rather than synthetic, in character. As conceived by the pioneers, the psychology of religion could be the analytic study. Synthesis could then be made by theology on matters of truth, by ethics on matters of right, and by religious education or pastoral theology on what to do about it. But was this a sound assumption? Suppose that the study of history, which begins with analysis, were to be cut off after the analysis was made; and the function of suggesting the constructive implications were left entirely to philosophy on the theoretical side and to education on the practical side? In that event, few people who accepted such a working definition of history would devote a major part of their time to the field. They, too, would want to become philosophers or educators.

We receive confirmation of this point from the word "of" in the psychology of religion. This suggests mere analysis. So long as the field is conceived to involve analysis alone—hence to imply either reductionism or a rigid separation of the analytical from the constructive functions—so long will it fail to develop as a field of study. This is exactly what has happened.

So we have the paradox that the psychological understanding of religion has developed very considerably, but the centre and original source of the field has remained almost without development. Instead of finding their focus properly in the psychological understanding of religion, the new growths have seen themselves as having different foci, more or less unrelated to one another. We shall consider these new developments in turn, beginning with the philosophical stream or context, which has had by far the greatest number of voices.

In the philosophical group we see first the psychologists who have attempted to apply psychology to the understanding of religion and who, in the process, have decided that the really important question to be answered is: Does psychology demonstrate the truth or falsity of this or that about religion?

The earliest work of this kind was on the negative side, with J. H. Leuba (1921) leading the lists. To him religion might be a necessary stage in social evolution, but mature people would certainly get over it if they had the inside psychological dope, especially if they got a whiff of its psychogenesis. Sigmund Freud (1928) held a similar view, best expressed in *The Future of an Illusion*. He considered religion to be a form of obsessional neurosis, generalizing from the undoubted fact that it was so in some of the persons he saw. In a personal communication to John G. Greene in this country, in reply to a question whether he knew that religion here was often different from what Freud himself considered religion to be, Freud wrote that it saddened him to see many able Americans using time and energy on religion when otherwise they might be engaged in important service for social betterment. Freud professed himself to be antiphilosophical in general, but his views on religion are philosophical in character.[3]

It is not without interest that, for a number of years, the University of Iowa group in psychology was perhaps the most obviously reductionist group of psychological students of religion in a university centre. Under the guise of natural science method, narrowly interpreted and mechanically applied, they gave vent to anti-Bible-belt feelings in a way which probably guaranteed a maximum of safety. It is further notable that Edwin D. Starbuck, who

---

[3] Sigmund Freud (1930). Reducing religion was one of the chief preoccupations of the German magazine, *Imago*, a Freudian journal founded about 1912.

had started the whole thing off, was associated with this group. He must have been unhappy at the shading off of his natural science study by others into philosophical channels. If so, his group took a most unpsychological and most unfruitful way to get it back into what they felt was midstream.

The antireligionists were at least balanced, however, by the proreligionists. Oskar R. Pfister, one of Freud's earliest followers and a psychoanalytic practitioner, was a Swiss minister. It is something of a mystery why Pfister has been so little known in America. Had he written more stridently, doubtless he would have been translated earlier. His works which have found their way into English appeared so late that their circulation has been handicapped. While not strikingly original, they deserve more serious attention than they have yet received.[4]

The record shows, however, that few persons who could be called psychologists by any reasonable stretch of the imagination turned their attention to religion in a sympathetic manner before the 1920's. After the first world war, especially in view of the prestige which psychology gained during the war, more attacks were made on religion from the psychological point of view; and these were followed by psychological defenses.

William McDougall can probably be considered such an apologist though most of his works touching on religion have appeared in comparatively recent years. So, in a neutral kind of way, may we call Adolf Meyer.[5] Despite McDougall's expansive and impressive theorizing, his work leaves the impression of a discursive essayist rather than that of a systematic observer, basic thinker, or constructive philosopher. Adolf Meyer and his multitude of followers, who called themselves "psychobiologists," have performed an extremely important function in psychiatric history by breaking down much prejudice against seeing psychological factors as being as real as physiological factors. But in their desire to be inclusive, they lost sharpness of definition. As one psychiatrist has said, they failed to see the trees for the forest. Yet in a day when many psychological thinkers were against religion as such, the Meyer school had at least the virtue of not attacking it every time it appeared in a patient or an idea. They accepted it as a fact of life. And yet, because they failed to develop an adequate constructive theoretical point of view, their views on a study of religion have not been fruitful. A recent book by H. J. Simpson (1945), a clergyman, written entirely from the Meyer point of view, demonstrates this clearly.

With the 1920's there came a rash of works to defend Christianity against the onslaughts of psychology, such as that of F. R. Barry (1923, 1923a). Harrison S. Elliott (1927) offered a defense, but pointed out at the same time that Christianity could not ignore the findings of psychology. J. A. Hadfield

[4] See Oskar R. Pfister (1928, 1944, 1963).
[5] Despite his acknowledged leadership of the so-called school of psychiatry for nearly forty years, Adolf Meyer has written no books, only occasional articles.

(1925), writing with a deceptive simplicity, was popular especially at a period when many religionists were inclined to regard religion as "morality touched with emotion." Sir William Brown (1929) and several other British psychologists or psychiatrists took up the cudgels against Ernest Jones and other psychoanalytic philosophers. The best of these works was by J. G. McKenzie (1929) the Scottish social scientist. These works were of various degrees of quality, but they were all apologetic. If religion had not been under attack from some psychological quarters, one wonders how many of them would have written psychology at all.

In the 1930's several religious psychologists also turned apologists. Henry Nelson Wieman and Regina Westcott Wieman (1935) presented a psychological buttress to their philosophy of theistic naturalism. J. D. Hollington (1938) attempted to reassure moralistic religionists that psychology would not cut off their heads. Karl R. Stolz (1923, 1932, 1937, 1939, 1943) published several books whose major theme was apologetic, and which urged religious people to use the insights of psychology for religious purposes; unfortunately both the psychology and theology involved lacked depth.

It is possible that therapeutic psychologists like Carl G. Jung and Fritz Kunkel should be considered as philosophers. Our discussion will, however, consider them in a later section.

Thus far we have considered the persons whose primary orientation was psychological, who turned their psychological knowledge on religion not for the purpose of understanding how it operates but to attack or·defend it in a theological sense. We may now look at the attempts by theologians and religious philosophers to pay special attention to the impact of the psychological understanding of religion upon our general understanding of religion. Few theologians in recent years have failed to make some reference to psychology, but the reference here is to those who have given the subject serious study.

At least two of W. E. Hocking's (1912, 1923) major works, though essentially philosophical in character, bore the marks of discriminating acquaintance with psychology. Harald Hoeffding's (1906) work defining religion in terms of valuation made good use of such psychology as was available at the time of its publication. W. R. Inge (1909), in an attempt to demonstrate the primary character of religion, rooted it in a "deep-seated religious instinct or impulse." This point has by now gone out the front door—though one has a suspicion that it has been brought in again through the back door by Jung and Kunkel. L. W. Grensted (1930) was another British preacher and theologian who defended religion against psychology.

Walter M. Horton's (1931) interesting excursion into the psychological field came in the early thirties. He was chiefly concerned to demonstrate that no empirical psychology could make the basic experiencing of religion irrelevant, and he chose worship around which to centre his discussion, attempting to prove the objective character of worship even after all the factors mentioned by psychologists were taken into account.

Several volumes by a British professor, T. Hywell Hughes (1933, 1937, 1937a, 1941, 1942) belong in the philosophical category although the subject matter is largely psychological. The general idea is that psychology which considers religion untrue or irrelevant because of its genesis is wrong. The idea is good but the books are undistinguished.

Several other religious philosophers and theologians have given major attention to psychological facts and points of view, such as Stewart Woodburn (1927) and Edwin E. Aubrey (1940). A recent extended article by Paul Tillich (1946) examines the underlying bases in theology and in dynamic psychology and compares them. The writings of such other theologians as Edgar S. Brightman, Reinhold Niebuhr, H. Richard Niebuhr, William Temple, Robert L. Calhoun, Nicholas Berdyaev, and others, have devoted attention to certain aspects of psychology in relation to religion, though not always with equal insight or helpfulness. The recent interest in Soren Kierkegaard has called attention to such matters as the meaning of anxiety, in large part a psychological question whether so recognized by the theologians or not. It remains true at present, however, that most theologians are inclined to regard psychology more as an enemy than a friend if they consider it relevant at all, and to interpret their function in relation to it as establishing reality or objectivity in contrast to the subjectivizing tendencies they feel are inherent in psychology. Indeed, it is not uncommon to find theologians who use the terms "psychology" and "subjective" almost interchangeably.

It is clear that a Christian apologetic is needed against psychology or anything else which professes to attack one or more of the roots of Christianity. Hence, there is an important theological and philosophical function to be performed against the psychologizing of religion out of existence or to a place of irrelevance. But this cannot be effective or enduring if done by people of limited competence, or if done by those who, despite competence in philosophy, do not take the trouble to be competent also in psychology. Only a small proportion of our leading religious philosophers today have a sufficient acquaintance with psychology to defend psychologically what needs and deserves defense in Christianity.

It is troubling to find that most theologians seem interested to defend Christianity at any particular time only against that which secularists feel threatens it. Twenty years ago secularists felt Christianity was seriously threatened by psychology; so the theologians took up the battle. Today the main apologetic battle ground is in the arena of politics (and of the politics of economics). This is truly of first importance, but should not imply no attention to psychology. Too many theologians are content to pay but passing attention to psychology, under the illusion that the issues are already settled or that psychology is of no importance. Lacking psychological knowledge, they face the temptation of accepting a psychology whose author says he agrees with their Christian assumptions, whether the psychological facts involved are true or not. More than one theologian accepts the psychology of Fritz Kunkel because he has avowedly Christian assumptions, and of Carl G. Jung because he does not deny Christian assumptions—without any apparatus for judging the psychology itself which is professedly based on these assumptions. This situation can be a great danger to theology. Serious study of the psychological understanding of religion by theologians would be an asset to theology.

THE NORMATIVE STREAM

Beginning with the study of the psychology of religion, we have discussed two of the streams which are its lineal descendants—the ever smaller and less significant main stream repeating the pattern of the pioneers, and the philosophical stream. The third is the educational or normative stream.

At the turn of the century those trends emerged in the field of secular education of which John Dewey was the acknowledged prophet. They were psychological trends in the sense that they were interested in what happened within the child or person who was experiencing the educative process. In the early years of the century Dewey was "psychologically wise." Recently, however, in an article tracing the development of Dewey's psychological thinking, Gordon W. Allport (Schilp, 1939) pointed out that Dewey had permitted this to remain relatively static, and suggested that his philosophy and educational theory would have been greatly strengthened if he had taken new findings and viewpoints in psychology into account. Dewey acknowledged that this was correct, that he had permitted his psychology to remain less examined than any other aspect of his thinking. And yet Dewey had kept himself on familiar terms with much that was appearing in the psychological field.

Something similar seems to have occurred in the field of Christian education. Despite all the misunderstandings and cleavages which have been caused by having a good part of the modern religious education movement develop outside and out of sympathy with the churches, the reasons for this development are understandable. For it must be remembered that, against a background of Biblicism and revivalism and airy idealism and even obscurantism, men like King and Coe in the early years of the century represented the kind of intelligence which would have rebelled against these at any time. They were quick to look favorably upon the trends in educational theory which Dewey was stimulating, at the same time maintaining the Christian perspective which Dewey renounced. More than one church leader at this time was talking euphorically of saving the world in one generation. George A. Coe must have been more than a little skeptical of such optimism, and even more of the kind of methodology by which such desirable results were to be achieved. People like Coe wanted to reach large numbers of people, just as the others did; but were convinced that this was not possible unless they were recognized as individuals. So it was natural for them to conclude that the only approach which really had a chance of getting to large numbers was an educational one, based on Christian truth, but containing in its method the genius of the Dewey approach—that people learn in proportion as they recognize their interests to be touched.

The religious educators of the early part of the century were not blind optimists. They did not know how far they could get in applying the new methods. But what they saw too often was a large ecclesiastical institution going through evangelistic and educational motions uncritically, using methods which could not possibly succeed in doing what the institution wanted to have done. Small wonder that they went to work on their own instead of waiting for orders from the theologians or church leaders.

The religious education movement, feeling more kinship with secular progressive education than with much of the then-current theological and ecclesiastical thinking, outdid itself in trying to achieve independence—in much the same way an adolescent tries to become independent of his parents. It was then promptly put on the spot, and the net effect was to make most of the professional religious educators into philosophers of a sort—exponents of a philosophy of development. Most of the movement's leaders became so drawn into such philosophy that they failed to do the work on procedures of application even of their own philosophy which would have been necessary to qualify them as practical experts. For a time they thought religious education was going to become a large profession independent of the ministry; and there it would find its professional constituency and the strength wherewith it could challenge what it felt to be the authoritarian assumptions of the theologians and ecclesiastics.

Now the religious education situation has changed radically. One may welcome the reintegration of religious education with theology, and its remarriage as a movement with the churches. But it is distressing to view the losses which have gone hand in hand with these gains, such as the fact that hardly anywhere in this country are people being trained for work in religious education above the level required to direct a local church program.

These general words about religious education have been necessary as a preliminary to what follows, how the development of religious education has been related to the psychological understanding of religion. It now seems clear that religious education treated psychology in about the same way John Dewey did, accepting and using its findings at the beginning of the century but later failing to pay serious attention to new findings. For example, the early work on the religious conversion of adolescents suggested that sudden conversions were not necessarily a desirable phenomenon, from which the implication could be drawn that different patterns of religious education could achieve improved results with fewer pains. But when psychology later discovered some things which tended to qualify that conclusion, it was natural for religious educators to pay lip service to the new finding but to stick to the old. Acceptance of a new truth is not proof against dogmatism; it merely alters the possibilities of what a dogmatism can contain. When the antimoralism that was contained in therapeutic psychology came into the picture, bringing with it a threat to views on character education, religious educators made a bow to it, acknowledged that the insights were important, but generally continued to treat religious education as if it were equivalent to moral education.

And yet the professional religious educators did pay attention to the understanding of religion through psychological means long before the theologians had interest in this. It was they who first brought psychology into the theological curriculum.

It is no exaggeration to suggest that the swing by George A. Coe from work in the psychology of religion to work in religious education is the most important single datum to be considered under this section. His move was a great loss to the cause of the psychological understanding of religion. Barring his lack of knowledge of dynamic psychology, most of which developed after he left the field of religious psychology, he had all the equipment necessary to make a definitive contribution to this field. His move has been beneficial to religious education; but it is possible that he could have done even religious education more good by majoring in religious psychology.

Harrison S. Elliott (1936, 1941) deserves special mention. More than any other among the religious educators, he has kept reminding his colleagues that they must ground their work more solidly in the growing knowledge of psychological understanding of religion. He has also pioneered in the application of the insights of therapeutic psychology.

Most of the leaders in religious education accepted what might be called the initial insights of the psychology of religion, and thought they were accepting later insights as these emerged. As a matter of fact, a real acceptance of some of the later ones would have made it essential to qualify earlier ones. To be vital and to renew vitality, religious education must drink at two springs, those of theology and of psychology. Its failure to drink deeply at either spring until recently has made it dry. At present the water from the theological spring is being dumped on it as from a barrel, with the one unfortunate and unnecessary result that it is rapidly approaching contemporary theology in its lack of interest in psychology. Perhaps it was good for religious education to lose its life as a thing apart. But as the defender and interpreter, for thirty years, of psychology to the theologians, it helped to injure theology as well as weaken itself by failing to pay more than lip service to changing approaches in religious psychology.

THE NATURAL SCIENCE STREAM

After its liberation from the chains of rationalistic philosophy and its experimental flutters with empirical method, general psychology discovered there was gold in the hills of natural science. As demonstrated in the early work of Starbuck, even narrowly interpreted natural science could have significance in fostering psychological understanding of religion. If scientific method was conceived too narrowly, if statistics and questionnaires and quantities were sometimes mistakenly equated with science, this does not prove that such methods are not potentially fruitful even though their potential significance is far from all-embracing.

The work of Hugh Hartshorne (1933) is perhaps the best illustration of the kind of results which are possible in the application of natural science methods to the psychological understanding of religion. It is not without significance that most of Hartshorne's findings on character, for example, seemed to have negative connotations, i.e., they proved that certain illusions needed to be discarded. Such knowledge is of great value, but those who produce it are not often rewarded.

Ernest J. Chave (1937, 1939) is another who has applied natural science methods to the psychological understanding of religion. The significance of his findings has not, however, been properly assessed because he has attached an empiricist philosophy to his empirical findings.

Ernest M. Ligon (1935, 1940) is another who has attempted to use natural science methods in understanding religion psychologically. His first volume attempted to apply psychology to understanding the teachings of Jesus, without much knowledge of New Testament times and with a psychology which had only small traces of dynamic elements. This second book on religion reports his experience as psychological consultant to a local church school, where the paraphernalia of tests and records are used. Whatever the objective value of the tests and records, they bring the prestige of science to the church school, and seem to be an unparalleled way of getting parents interested in their children.

If one looks further for concrete material along natural science lines, he will find a welter of B.D. and A.M. dissertations, an occasional doctor's thesis, but rarely any study using natural science methods that makes a significant contribution to the psychological understanding of religion. And we find this in the United States where we are accused of overdoing this type of study.

In studying articles over a number of years in the *Journal of Religion* as a representative scholarly magazine of religion, Anton T. Boisen found that only a small proportion of the articles referred in any significant way to empirical material, and an infinitesimal number reported results of the natural science approach. It is time, therefore, that this particular ghost is laid. One does not have to be an empiricist to believe that empirical investigation can be fruitful; and one does not have to believe that natural science methods must be applied to psychological investigation without change in order to be convinced that such methods, properly adapted, have important though limited possibilities in our attempt to gain a psychological understanding of religion. Why have not even the empiricists produced much, good or bad, which comes from empirical investigation?

The obvious reason is that people who operate as professionals in the field of religion have to produce the good whereby people can live, and it requires more than a little perspective and discipline to be both a scientist and a helper or educator at the same time. Many aspire but few seem to make the grade.

Another reason has been the narrow perfectionism about what scientific method is, to which students of religion have not been immune. One may become so preoccupied with method, put his methodological standards so high, or set them up so rigidly, that the conditions which would be required to meet them make any concrete study practically impossible. A few of the most promising students have allowed this to happen to them.

Actually, scientific method in this field must do one of two things. On the one hand, it can make its area of investigation extremely narrow, and then proceed like other investigations in the social or psychological sciences. In that case the findings will be definite but will cover only a narrow area; hence most theologians will pay little attention to them. On the other hand, it can cut a wider swathe, using scientific method for some aspect of the study, but adapting it as practical questions arise. If this is done, then the methodists of natural science will deny that the work is scientific, but the theologians may pay attention to it. A variant of this is to use scientific method for part of the study, and then frankly move on to other aspects of the question to which similar data are not available or relevant. But so long as the perfectionistic spirit prevails, we are not likely to witness many helpful contributions to the psychological understanding of religion from natural science methods.

Projective tests developed by clinical psychology in recent years offer considerable promise in helping to answer some of the obscure questions in the psychological understanding of religion, notably typological questions. What is involved in that type of personality structure, for example, which feels almost equally drawn to Quakerism and Anglo-Catholicism? Or, does the kill-or-cure type of disturbing religious experience tend to occur with certain patterns of personality, or is its precipitation more dependent upon types of social situation? These are important questions which the proper use of projective test can help answer, though little seems to have been done as yet.

The ultimate findings from the natural science approach, if conceived narrowly, will probably not be far-reaching, but collectively they may be important. And if, in connection with the use of natural science method, there is translation of its meaning and not merely transliteration, the significance of the findings may be much greater.

THE THERAPEUTIC OR DYNAMIC STREAM

Dynamic psychology originated in the therapist's office, not in the classroom or the laboratory. The persistent questions which gave rise to it were not theoretical but practical, not philosophical but clinical, not normative but therapeutic. The interest which lay behind its initiation, therefore, was like that of the pastor in contrast to that of the scholar or theologian. Whatever the importance theoretically of the questions involved, something new was needed to help people who wanted to be helped. In the process of finding what would give practical help, new veins of theoretical ore were struck.

In discussing Freud, one always runs the danger of accepting important discoveries without acknowledgement, or even without knowing how original they were when promulgated, and spending most of one's time criticizing Freud for the things one does not like. So far as can be seen now, however, the three major and permanent contributions of Freud are those enunciated by Karen Horney (1939). There is first the point "that psychic processes are strictly determined." As intended here, it means that any particular act of behavior has antecedents and is largely traceable, and that no act of behavior is merely capricious. The second point is "that actions and feelings may be determined by unconscious motivations," that is, that forces properly to be viewed as psychological in nature, outside the field where they have capacity for entrance into consciousness by ordinary means, nevertheless influence the total activity and conscious awareness and sensitized perceptions of the individual involved. Third, "that the motivations driving us are emotional forces," that is, that the driving forces of human life can be understood only in a context of struggle and conflict, of needs and frustrations, of feelings rather than ideas except insofar as ideas represent needs or aspects of conflicts. Freud attached certain theoretical contents to these points which are not necessary accompaniments. But they are the cardinal principles upon which all dynamic psychologies rest, and they stem from Freud.

Reference has already been made to Freud's philosophical attitude to religion, which was clearly reductionist. The significance of the three points named above, however, is quite different for the psychological understanding of religion. To believe securely that behavior, including religious behavior, has antecedents can free us from the tyranny of capriciousness in attempting to interpret the way in which religion operates. It can give us the key, for example, to understanding the depth of the experience of many alcoholics as their lives are changed through joining Alcoholics Anonymous.

It can enable us, on psychological grounds, to challenge the assertion of the superficial psychiatrists that the experience does not reach deep because it does not start with genetic insights. As another example, it can give us the base from which we can discover what the connection is between the drawing power of Anglo-Catholicism and Quakerism—rather than merely considering it a matter of taste that some persons are attracted to both.

Similarly, the reality of unconscious motivations opens up new fields for understanding religion psychologically. Why is it that the Southern Baptists and the Roman Catholics are in a neck-and-neck race in a certain Southern town, with only a hair's breadth seeming to decide whether certain people join one church or the other? How is it that so many people who have a penchant for the more abstract forms of religious philosophy are also interested in music? How is it that so many people who try desperately hard to express love are unable to do so until they first confront their own hatred? The questions are endless, and Freud has supplied a base upon which answers may be secured.

That the driving forces of human life are emotional in nature is of great significance for religion. Life is not an easy march up a slight hill, with harmony and lack of conflcit the marks of a successful climb. Life itself is dynamic. Even the most exalted philosopher does not altogether chart his own course. One may be a captain of one's soul, perhaps, but one is still in an army with five-star generals. The question then becomes not whether one will "adjust" but to what in the universe and in himself he will "adjust." This point has kinship with Schleiermacher's "absolute dependence," though it is not the same. Another way to put it is that man and men must come to something in their nature as human beings, and this must be seen on a human and psychological as well as on a biological level.

This is not to suggest that these are the implications Freud intended us to draw. But the fact is that his contributions provide a base from which these implications may be drawn, and the latter are profoundly important for the psychological understanding of religion.

It is even more difficult to discuss Jung than Freud. Jung is an emotional subject. Either he is considered to be the great white father of a new way of thinking and feeling which comes close to being a religion, or else he is a seducer of men's souls. From the point of view of the psychological understanding of religion, however, there are at least two major permanent contributions which belong to Jung (1916, 1923, 1928, 1933, 1938, 1939). First, he has demonstrated that the contents of the unconscious are not necessarily bad or harmful, but may be more constructive and creative than the conscious side of the personality. There is something in persons which demands to be let out, however great the obstacles which bind it, and it cannot be understood except in human terms. Thus Jung can see repression as "a sort of half-conscious and half-hearted letting go of things, a dropping of hot cakes or a reviling of grapes which hang too high." This is significant for the psychological understanding of religion; for stoicism is not then required in order to be willing to explore the contents of the unconscious. The theistic naturalist would say that this gives the Holy Spirit a place in nature. The supernaturalist would say it demonstrates the process whereby Divine Grace enters human life.

Jung's second major contribution is this: psychic ill-health can best be understood from the point of view of bias or one-sidedness. Jung never lets up on the intellectual who refuses to act except through the dictates of his head. It might be called the all-your-eggs-in-one-basket theory of neurosis. In contrast to illness, Jung sees psychic health in people who are in communication with a considerable part of the totality of themselves and not merely with a limited and overspecialized segment. This, too, is of importance for the psychological understanding of religion, especially in understanding resistances to religion. This gives us a sounder clue than Freud gave, for example, to the nature and meaning of obsessive rituals in intellectuals who have renounced religion. It also enables us to face up to the necessity of taking people's introspections and dreams and other projections seriously as phenomena which may possess religious significance.

With all of this Jung has included some speculations which, while always interesting, are not invariably helpful, and we shall charitably refrain from mentioning them. But Jung is in no sense naïve philosophically as Freud was. He wrote, for instance: "The thing that cures a neurosis must be as convincing as the neurosis; and since the latter is only too real, the helpful experience must be of equal reality. It must be a very real illusion, if you want to put it pessimistically. But what is the difference between a real illusion and a healing religious experience?" (1938, p. 114). We can reply that there is a difference to the philosopher and theologian; but as a psychological student of religion Jung is perfectly correct in assuming the right to take a position of metaphysical agnosticism.

The irritating thing about Jung is those among his devoted followers who have generalized on the psychology involved in their own healing experience, and who have sometimes created a metaphysical system out of what Jung seems to have intended to be only a psychology. Jung is also misleading because he apparently refuses to take sociology and cultural anthropology seriously. But none of these things should prevent us from seeing and using his permanent contributions.

Fritz Kunkel (1936, 1938, 1940, 1943) who was not originally but who has now become a Jungian, may be considered next. Unlike Jung, he is personally and publicly committed to Christianity. He is an inveterate user of paradoxes, is invariably interesting and usually penetrating. He is a Christian Jung, minus the more abstruse mythology. But his gift for paradox and concept gets such a tight hold on him that at times he becomes addicted to gross generalizations and exaggerations which may obscure rather than clarify what psychology has to contribute to the understanding of religion.

While it is difficult to assess the total contribution of Otto Rank because of his obscure style, one point of special significance to the psychological understanding of religion can be easily stated. It involves Rank's effort to restate the meaning of "will." [6] As used in the old faculty psychology, the concept became meaningless when the foundations of psychology became empirical and then dynamic. Those who came before Rank were content to denounce will in the old framework, apparently feeling that the whole problem might then be dropped. Rank recognized that acceptance of the three Freudian and two Jungian points mentioned here made it imperative to find some way of discussing inner conative strivings—and he rightly felt that this was akin to "will," even though the implications of the term in its new setting were quite different from those of the old setting, symbolized in the phrase "will-power." Will in Rank's sense was not distinguished by conscious purpose, but by personality movement; it might or might not get into consciousness. This point has importance for understanding religion; for it provides a base for understanding purpose in human and individual life as something deeper and broader than consciousness. Thus, for example, no later treatise professing to deal with psychological understanding of religion can call itself *Religious Consciousness*.

Rank's theory of will is also important in terms of actually helping people. It is he, more than any other modern psychotherapist, who has been able, without any depreciation of the strength of the obstacles and negative forces in the psyche, to assert the capacity of the personality to take initiative in finding its own way if given half a chance. Thus, Rank's theoretical work may be considered, for example, to be the chief prerequisite for Carl R. Rogers' (1939, 1942, 1946) methods in psychotherapy.

The later Freudians and neo-Freudians have also made some contributions of permanent value to the psychological understanding of religion. Franz Alexander (1930, 1946) has contributed a clearer elaboration from the empirical point of view of the nature of the self, with particular reference to the way in which aspects of the self may be used as objects by other aspects of the self. The understanding of what is involved in self-punishment is vital to religious psychology. Karl A. Menninger (1937, 1938, 1942) has followed through on this, more clearly and understandably than Alexander, but without the latter's philosophical equipment. Menninger deserves further mention not so much because of originality of theory as because of his wide influence as the best known exponent of modified Freudianism. More than any other current psychological writer, he has driven home to preachers and the general intellectual public the reality and power of the darker aspects of psychic

---

[6] See especially Otto Rank (1929, 1932, 1936, 1936a).

life, "the kingdom of evils," to use the term of Menninger's teacher Southard (1922). Menninger's mechanism and instinctualism make him an unsafe guide in matters of theory, but he has an extraordinary capacity for clarifying complex psychological matters.

The controversy still rages as to whether Karen Horney's (1937, 1939, 1945) ideas are hers, or whether she merely was the first to put in print things which many in the Freudian tradition had been thinking. At any rate she was the first to put these things before the public. The major contribution involves the relation of personality patterns to cultural pressures.[7] To treat psychic ill-health as if it were a mere sport due to individual idiosyncrasies was clearly inadequate from the point of view of the social origin of personality. True, the social psychologists (and George Herbert Mead) had said this before, but not on the basis of an intimate knowledge of individual psychological dynamics. This point is of obvious importance to the psychological understanding of religion. To be able to understand inner psychic conflicts as the resultants of conflicting pressures within the culture—as these are adopted as aspects of the self—is to make comprehensible the production of psychic conflicts without being tempted to biological reductionism. There remains the danger of sociological reductionism, but that bubble is more easily burst.

In her more recent works, Horney has further clarified the nature and genesis of the forces at work in inner conflicts. Here the contribution to the psychological understanding of religion is not so much theoretical as it is related to specific psychic contents, for example, aiding in the psychological analysis of love and the obstacles to it. Without minimizing Horney's contribution, one regrets that she has thus far limited her implications to specific analytical statements and has not also suggested the constructive and creative implications of her work and point of view.

Harry Stack Sullivan, like Rank, has obscured his contribution to general knowledge by an abstruse and complex style.[8] Similar to Horney in his thinking, he is more impressed with the importance of studying the particular points at which aspects of culture are mediated to the individual than with the more abstracted analysis of the culture itself. Thus he speaks of "the psychology and biology of interpersonal relationships." Considered by some to be the most brilliant psychiatric thinker in America, it may be hoped that he will publish the essentials of his point of view some day in book form.

Erich Fromm (1947) occupies a position closely similar to that of Horney and Sullivan, but his special concern is with the relation of dynamic psychol-

[7] Another valuable contribution to the same point was published about the same time, James S. Plant (1938).
[8] Harry Stack Sullivan's writings may be found throughout the publication history of *Psychiatry*, issued by the William Alanson White Foundation, of which Sullivan has been the directing head.

ogy to ethics and philosophy. Rank's point that there is something within personality which has a striving and purposive quality is accepted by Fromm, but more careful analysis of its nature is felt to be required. Fromm may be said to be interested in the development of what might be called a "metaphysics of the psyche," drawn from empirical sources, as contrasted either with thoughtless empiricism on the one hand or "objective metaphysics" on the other. His contribution to the psychological understanding of religion is showing that there is what I, not he, have called a "metaphysics of the psyche," which psychologists must take into account, whether they are interested in metaphysics in the ordinary sense or not.

For a considerable time the only psychologists who paid adequate attention to the dynamic and individuating elements in personality were the therapists, and nearly all of these were medical men. Within the past ten years personality psychology has become a respectable subject for non-medical psychologists as seen especially in the outstanding work of Gordon Allport (1937, 1944), and in that of such men as Henry A. Murray (1938, 1943), Ross Stagner (1937), P. M. Symonds (1931, 1939), Kurt Lewin (1935, 1936, 1938) and many others. Most of them have adopted what have been noted herein as the most basic points brought out by the therapeutic psychologists; and there seems to be a close connection between the importance they attach to these points and the degree to which they have a therapeutic as well as a scientific truth interest.

The movement in non-medical psychology leading to an interest in personality psychology has been helped along considerably by the Gestalt or configurationist movement in general psychology led by Kurt Koffka (1924, 1935), Wolfgang Köhler (1929, 1942) and Kurt Lewin. The Gestalt movement rebelled against geneticism in all its forms, pointed out that the whole is a great deal more than the sum of its parts, and pointed out that functionally a man's eye had a closer relationship to his own nose than it had to the eye of someone else. In essence, it was a new viewpoint on perception. Its essential message has been incorporated into general psychology, and has been especially fruitful when linked with dynamic and therapeutic psychology. It has made an important contribution to the bases upon which religious psychology can rest, by disclosing the fallacies involved in geneticist and reductionist types of psychological thinking and perceiving.

Carl R. Rogers was the first of the non-medical psychologists to challenge effectively the domination of the field of therapeutic psychology by the medical group. In the process he had to construct a psychology of therapy based on minimum essentials in contrast to all the previous theories of therapy, which were based on maximum goals. At first Rogers seemed to suggest that a knowledge of dynamic psychology was no help, and might be a handicap, in the therapeutic process. But since he is no obscurantist, he has recently modified what seemed to be his earlier position. His major contribution is in the field of procedures, not theory; but in his demonstration of the implications of Rank's point—what it really means to trust the movement of the inner constructive forces of the personality—he has confounded many who accepted this point in general but failed to follow it in practice.[9] Thus he has put methodological meat on Rank's theoretical bones. From the point of view of the psychological understanding of religion, Rogers has made available new and learnable procedures for studying the inner forces that, with a bit of help from the therapist, make for integration and reintegration of the personality.

Thus far our discussion has concerned the leaders in the field of therapeutic psychology and the new bases which their work has made possible in the field of psychological understanding of religion. We now turn to some of the leaders in the religious field who have attempted to apply the insights of therapeutic or dynamic psychology to the actual understanding of religion. Under the section on philosophy we have already pointed out how many of the persons who set out to do this landed in the philosophical field instead. This is not said in disparagement of the philosophical task, but to make clear that there is a different field which also requires exploration, namely what dynamic psychology demonstrates about the actual functioning of religion.

In Great Britain nearly all the material has moved in a philosophical direction, as demonstrated notably in the publications of the Guild of Pastoral Psychology.[10] Jung is much more widely followed in Britain than in America, and he is near to being the patron saint of the Guild. On the Continent there has been no published work in this field for some years, the reasons being too obvious to require mention. One must admit that a modicum of detachment is necessary in order to pursue study of the psychological understanding of religion.

Perhaps the most unique work in this field in America has been done by Anton T. Boisen (1936). While Boisen has not entirely resisted the temptation to become a philosopher, his main work remains in the psychological field. He has made empirical studies of the crisis type of psychological experience both in the mental hospital and among the holy-roller types of religious groups. He concludes that intellectual insight is not the major factor in determining whether the outcome of a disturbance will be a higher (religious) adjustment or a descent into psychopathological vegetation. In a still unpublished work Boisen has attempted to integrate the findings of his psychological and sociological studies of the dynamics of crisis experience with certain other observations on customs, *mores,* and loyalties. Be-

---

[9] Cf. the very considerable alternation of the conception of psychotherapy from the psychoanalytic point of view represented in Alexander (1930, 1946).

[10] The Guild of Pastoral Psychology is an English association of individuals, which holds meetings and publishes papers in pamphlet form.

cause of Boisen's own psychotic experience and certain preoccupations in his thinking, he has never received the attention his work deserves. In his study of religious experience in psychotics, as well as in his dynamic study of eruptive forms of group religious experience, he has broken entirely new ground, and eventually his findings will have to be taken seriously.

Carroll A. Wise (1942) has made a commendable effort to synthesize the essential findings of dynamic psychology as they are relevant to the understanding of religion. His summary of dynamic psychology, psychosomatic medicine, and related scientific subjects is especially competent. Concerning religion, he feels that the most fruitful approach to understanding it psychologically is through the medium of analysis of symbols in terms of their meaning in the life of individuals. He has carried this analysis through to a point where it becomes convincing, at least as one method of study of the psychological understanding of religion. Unfortunately he has not yet documented his work with the concrete material which could clarify the importance of his approach. He has further handicapped himself by not making clear enough his acquaintance with current trends in theological thinking, and as a result some theologians have mistakenly concluded that he is an empiricist, which he is not.

Ernest Hilgard's article (See Thomas, 1944) on "Christianity and Contemporary Psychology" shows that he has an important potential contribution to make to this field. He has taken dynamic psychology seriously into account, and he is not preoccupied entirely with philosophical questions. Thus far, however, he has given only an introduction to the subject.

J. G. McKenzie (1940), the Scottish social scientist, has recently tried a new tack. He starts with the assumption that previous attempts to understand religion psychologically have been abortive because they have failed to distinguish between major types of religious experience. He then sets out to define the evangelical type, and to apply psychology to understanding that particular type of experience. In the process, he not only admits that he considers the evangelical to be superior to other types of religious experience, but asserts that it is this fact which makes it possible for him to have psychological understanding of evangelical religious experience. While interesting, his work is general and on the abstract side, and to some extent falls into the category of apologetics.

J. A. C. Murray (1938), another Scotsman but a pastor not a professor, has attempted to make the point that the outcome of psychotherapy is almost entirely dependent upon the assumptions of the therapist, and that Christianity can work with psychotherapy only if it develops therapists with clear Christian assumptions. There is much to be said for Murray's main point. Unfortunately, however, he has only a very general notion of dynamic or therapeutic psychology, and persistently confuses psychology and philosophy. While his concern arises from therapeutic psychology, its application is not to the psychological understanding of religion nor even to therapy itself, but to theological conversion of psychotherapists.

In a recent volume Lewis J. Sherrill (1945) has attempted to assess and compare the findings and convictions of therapeutic psychology and of Christian theology in relation to the understanding of religious processes, with special reference to guilt and its cure. While the volume makes a definite theological point in line with the rediscovered orthodoxy of the American school, its major intent is to show that knowledge of both dynamic psychology (for understanding guilt) and Christian theology (for understanding redemption) is necessary to understanding and action in relation to the whole process.

There are comparatively few other religious writers who have attempted to apply the insights of therapeutic psychology to the understanding of religion in a nonpolemic or nonapologetic fashion. Harry Bone and Arthur Cushman McGiffert, Jr., did so briefly (See Hiltner, 1939). Most of the persons writing from the religious point of view about therapeutic psychology have rather naturally concentrated on the therapeutic and pastoral aspect. Thus Charles T. Holman (1932, 1942), John Sutherland Bonnell (1938), Leslie D. Weatherhead (1935), T. W. Pym (1922, 1925, 1928, 1930), Dewar and Hudson (1934), Russell L. Dicks (1936, 1945) and even Rollo May (1939, 1940), have centered their thought upon the implications of therapeutic or dynamic psychology for the practical work of the pastor. Certainly much work along this line, and not less, is needed.

So far Rollo May, with the exception of Paul E. Johnson, previously mentioned, is the only one of the pastoral group who has also felt it important to discuss the implications of therapeutic psychology for the understanding of religious processes. He has made some imaginative suggestions which are, however, not systematically organized, and the clarity of which is marred because he has tried to fulfill several different purposes in a single piece of writing.

It is clear that the major findings of therapeutic psychology have meaning for religion in more than one way. As Rollo May has clearly seen, they are important first for what they can teach concerning pastoral care and personal counseling. They are also important to theology and philosophy of religion; and the work done from this point on in that field, discussed briefly in the section above on philosophy, must take them more significantly into account than it has done in the past. They are important, thirdly, for the preacher, i.e., for the man who has to present spiritual food to people who need it. All of these have a "natural market" for writings drawing implications from dynamic psychology.

The market for material involving the psychological understanding of religion in a basic sense, however, is still a problem. Undoubtedly this fact is holding back work at the present time. If those groups mentioned above—

the pastors, theologians, and preachers—should recognize that the psychological understanding of religion is one of the bases on which they work, and that they need to study the fundamental implications for it of dynamic psychology and not merely in relation to their pragmatic interests—then a market might well develop which would lead to new and more significant work in the field.

ROMAN CATHOLIC AND JEWISH STUDY

There is no doubt that the psychological understanding of religion, as discussed here, is a Protestant affair. Both because of their authoritarianism in general and their specific dependence upon Thomism in particular, Roman Catholics have continued to treat modern psychological studies, especially dynamic types, with grave suspicion. It is difficult for Roman Catholic psychologists to make their work dynamic except in a purely methodological sense.

Rudolf Allers (1930, 1933, 1940) has taken up the cudgels against Freud, holding that because of Freud's theory and assumptions nothing about him could be accepted. Thomas Verner Moore (1926, 1943, 1944), a priest and a psychiatrist, has written several works from the Roman Catholic point of view having some reference to dynamic psychology. His volume *Dynamic Psychology* was suggestive, but none of his later writings have gone as far in recognizing the value and importance of this point of view.

Sante de Sanctis' (1927) work on conversion is one I have never had opportunity to examine. It is reported to be an attempt to fit conversion phenomena into an acceptable Thomistic pattern.

It is not without significance that the Roman Catholics have been as slow to apply the findings of therapeutic psychology to pastoral theology as they have to the psychological understanding of religion itself. Catholic social workers have applied the insights much more readily than have priests. Apologists will no doubt discover in a few years how to utilize some of the modern insights by pointing out that they were all implicit in historical teaching anyhow.

To the best of my knowledge, there are no Jewish religious books on the psychological understanding of religion written by experts in the religious field, unless one can so consider Liebman's (1946) work. Nor has this field been taught and cultivated in the Jewish theological schools, with the exception of Hebrew Union College where a psychiatrist-rabbi teaches it chiefly from the psychiatric point of view. The reasons for this are obscure. The Jewish group apparently feels that, where psychology is concerned, one should go to the professional psychologists; and this excludes rabbis since they are religionists. This is probably associated with the very different social role of the rabbi in the Jewish community as compared to that of either the Protestant minister or the Roman priest.

95

THE FUTURE

We live in a day when theology is being rediscovered, at least by the theologians, and we may hope that the discovery does not stop there. Collectively, we professional religionists seem to find it difficult to hold more than one interest at a time. When we are in the process of rediscovering Christian theology, then we seem unable to cast our attention to other jobs that also need doing. This despite the fact that when we see a similar trend in other professionals we get out the whip and give them a thrashing. Because medicine, for instance, is preoccupied with the enormously useful new pharmaceutical and mechanical discoveries, we sometimes tend to castigate the majority of doctors for being blind to what seem to us the equally important new discoveries in psychosomatic medicine. The patients need both; why must the doctors eschew one to be interested in the other? Let us put the shoe on our own foot—it fits.

Study of the psychological understanding of religion started in the period when natural science was assuming a commanding and even revolutionary place in the daily activities of men, at least so far as the use of its products was concerned. It reached its peak of interest at the time when uncritical optimism concerning the possibilities of natural science was at its height, and when concern about the whole range of theological reality was at its lowest modern point. Recently there has been more general agreement that science itself is neutral with regard to human welfare, and also a broadening of the range of theological concern. It is understandable that the original thrust in the direction of the psychological understanding of religion has nearly disappeared. But it will be tragic if something new and broader does not take its place; for now is the time when new tools and new insights give an enlarged study of the psychological understanding of religion far more potentialities than it ever had before.

We need to study the meaning and processes of religion from the psychological point of view for three basic reasons. The first is that people cannot be helped to discover and accept the resources of religion unless we understand what these actually mean in human life, which includes knowledge of what intends to block their acceptance. Second, we cannot have either an accurate or a meaningful theology if the psychological aspects of it are either uncriticized or are in naïve conflict with the best that is known in psychology. Third, we need to see the relation of processes involving religion to all psychological processes; so that psychology itself is recognized to be incomplete without an understanding of religion from the psychological point of view.

It is time, then, that at least three groups began to take seriously their obligation to study religion from the psychological point of view; the pastoral and educational group, the theological group, and the general psychological group. The first or practical group tends to be preoccupied with pragmatic results, and falsely relegates really basic material in this field entirely to the theologians. The theological group has considered psychological questions to be far down the list in importance, and yet it discusses many psychological questions without an adequate knowledge of psychology. The general psychology group is still so fearful of departing from the pure methods of natural science that it will not seriously ask the necessary questions.

At the present time the chief interest in the psychological understanding of religion is coming from the practical group. This is both sound and understandable. Throughout the Christian history it has usually been the leaders who had to produce the goods to help the people who have been most progressive and alert in their thinking, rather than those whose positions enabled them to be detached. Most of the practical leaders have been unable to put their insights into the systematic form requisite for posterity.

Today there are indications that this is happening again. The practical group is beginning to reach deeper than the pragmatic levels, to recognize that its field has a content as well as a method—and that this content is to be found in the insights of psychology and sociology used alongside the truth and resources of theology, and integrated with them. It is of no little interest that this concern is growing out of the therapeutic rather than the normative aspect of the practical field. The normative approach, as represented in religious education, had somehow been under the illusion that it could get along without either of the roots essential to it, psychology and sociology on the one hand, and theology on the other. It is now beginning to stage a recovery, but still seems so intent on keeping the wheels running that it has not yet taken time to reach beneath the surface.

Those who have had to help people in need, however, and who could not in conscience deny the obligation through applying labels like "abnormality" have begun to probe more deeply. Another way to put it is that clinical experience which is honest in its observations is bound to make people ask continually deeper questions—unless a premature preoccupation with ideological factors arbitrarily delimits the area in which the questions are asked. This fact is something more than incidental. It means that the most fruitful way of approaching the psychological understanding of religion is through the practical field, and through that therapeutic side of it which we are accustomed to call "pastoral" since its intent is shepherding.

If accepted generally, this would have several immediate practical applications. First, the initial study of the psychological understanding of religion on the part of students would be done in connection with clinical, or at least pastoral, studies—rather than merely as an aspect of study of theology and philosophy of religion. This is in contrast to the practice of many seminaries. Second, there would be a new recognition that the practical field has a content, not in contrast to the theological content but complementary to it. The practical field is not just a dealing with skills. Third, while commending the interest of theologians in the psychological understanding of religion, any attempts on their part to confine it merely to formal categories and systematic philosophies would be pointed to as biased.

At the same time, the psychological understanding of religion is of great importance for theology and the philosophy of religion. If the study of theology consists of God, man, sin, and salvation—then the kind of psychological understanding which is now becoming possible is related to all four fields. In other words, there is a sense in which psychological knowledge is an aspect of all theological knowledge. This is not to say, however, that the new creative insights of psychology can come about through merger with theology. For every time psychology has been taken as nothing but a part of theology, it has ceased to become creative. On the other hand, when psychological study has been divorced from theological study, it has taken refuge in resort to less consequential questions. Somehow psychology must be free to be creative and yet have its proper place as an asset of theological study. The first can be achieved by recognizing the chief source of creative insights to be in the clinical and pastoral procedures and reflections therefrom. The second can come from a study of theology which is willing to admit that its roots lie both in experience and in revelation, and which is sufficiently concerned with the experimental as well as the revelatory roots to study them concretely and not merely abstractly.

When we come to consider the types of concrete questions to which answers are most needed, and to the answering of which psychology can make the largest contribution, we may be struck anew by their breadth and importance. How do faith and doubt operate in the human psyche? Or love? Or conscience and the sense of guilt? What are the major typological factors involved in the experiencing of religion? Questions like these impinge upon every aspect of theological study. And the chief new creative insights which may help to answer them come potentially from the clinical or pastoral or therapeutic aspects of the practical field, rather than from philosophy or religious education or history or even from the sociological study of religion.

A further comment is required, however, on the sociology of religion or the sociological understanding of religion. This has never been a watertight compartment affair as has the psychology of religion. Its insights have been more freely merged with history, philosophy, and other approaches to understanding religion. It is now clear that lack of understanding of dynamics, which has characterized most of the work in the sociology of religion, must be remedied if it is to fulfill its promise. But if the dynamics are to be given their proper place, what is involved is a social psychology of religion, or a social psychological understanding of religion. Hence its future is more intimately tied up with that of the psychological understanding of religion than it has ever been in the past.

Some Trends in the Psychology of Religion

Paul W. Pruyser

Let me open with a quotation from a fellow psychologist, Gordon Allport: "A narrowly conceived science can never do business with a narrowly conceived religion. Only when both parties broaden their perspective will the way to understanding and cooperation open" (Allport, 1950, p. x). This is a very interesting statement in several ways. It tells us that, for the writer, science is not one thing but many and that religion is also not one thing but many. It says that we can have various attitudes toward science as well as toward religion. Such a critique can only be possible from a viewpoint well above science and religion, but whether there is any such vantage point, and what its name is, I cannot tell. Allport speaks further of science and religion "doing business with each other," and it strikes me that this does not quite fit with the cool and splendid detachment which my teachers told me was the attitude of scientists. And then he mentions this "broadening of perspective." Why should any discipline broaden its perspective? Is not psychology broad enough, and is it no longer true that religion deals with the whole universe, "while it groaneth and travaileth in pain"? And what about the "working together" of science and religion—is it merely because "togetherness" and "groupiness" are the catchwords of our time, or is there a scholarly interest in mutual learning and edification? If not, which other purpose could be served by such working together?

Despite their ring, these are not rhetorical questions. Consequently, they will not receive a rhetorical answer from me. Instead I shall try to give some comments on what I think has happened during the last fifty or sixty years in psychology and religion as these two have been brought into relation with each other. And I shall show in due time that Allport's statement makes eminent sense. I do so in the hope that an awareness of trends and developments may help us to find some sturdy footholds for further study. This will not be comprehensive but, for limitations of time and libido, only an elaborate sketch. I shall content myself with a few typical phases.

Let us first look at that rather specialized part of psychology which is called "psychology of religion." More than fifty years ago the leading academic psychologist in America at that time was asked to give the Gifford Lectures in Edinburgh. What William James (1902) said on that occasion constitutes probably still the most important single psychological work on

Reprinted from *Journal of Religion*, 40 (1960), 113-29. Copyright © 1960 by the University of Chicago Press.

99

religion. He made some excellent propositions: (a) that religious phenomena are continuous with other psychic phenomena; (b) that in religion, as everywhere else, the sublime and the ridiculous are two poles of a continuum, with a lot of ordinary, drab, and hackneyed happenings in between; (c) that in religion, as in other human endeavors, feelings tend to be more important than thoughts; (d) that there is not one single psychic wellspring for religion in the form of a special instinct, sentiment, or disposition; (e) that religion has a human and a divine side and that psychology can study only the former; and (f) that people do not simply *have* a God but that they *use* their God and that religion is known by its fruits in behavior. A little later, psychoanalytic investigators would repeat this last statement with more vigor and with a more precise knowledge of the kind of use people make of their God. James added a simple typology and had a keen interest in the medical side of religion, not only diagnostically, but also in terms of mental hygiene. That latter interest is again rearing its ugly head in our day (Meehl, 1957; Pruyser, 1958).

I believe that James's fourth point—that religion cannot be delegated to one special psychic function—is of major scientific importance. Before and after him many people have asked whether the essence of religious experience is to be found in a feeling, act, attitude, value, cognitive state, drive, or whatever. They sought an element, a *prima materia,* of religious experience. James's answer is the parallel in religion to the debunking of the old and outworn phlogiston theory in chemistry. *All* the psychological part processes may participate in religious experience, and *none* of them is specific to religion. Instead of raising the wrong question about specificity, let us inquire what the preponderant part processes are in the religious experience of certain people or in certain systems of religion; in other words, let us set forth the *varieties* of religious experience.

But, as soon as that inquiry has been made, one must raise the next question: whether the gist of religion really lies in part processes or whether it has to be sought elsewhere. If religion claims the whole man, as some of its spokesmen say, by what sort of process does it achieve its holistic, integrative character—if it ever does? James answered tentatively that this would involve a shift in the center of energy, but he could not pursue the matter in further detail.

There is some reason to wonder whether James's most lasting legacy, which led to the phenomenon known as the "James tradition," was not at bottom a political as well as a scientific contribution. After James the term "religious experience" has become an expression for a somewhat cagey way of dealing with certain aspects of the psychology of religion. Its premises seem to be: (a) some people have subjective experiences called "religious" of one sort or another; (b) psychology, as an empirical science, deals with experiences of people; therefore, (c) the psychology of religion, if it is to be empirical, deals with the subjective experiences of people called "religious."

There is nothing wrong with this conclusion, except that it is based upon too narrow a premise. For James, subjective experience meant feelings, and the best empirical data were to be found in the feelingful expressions of feelings. This emphasis on feeling and utter subjectivity cuts down on the importance of cognitive states, decisions, and acts—on the very things that systematic and moral theology is interested in. Hence the work of James and his followers needed not to be taken too seriously by the theological disciplines. After all, *this* psychology of religion dealt only with the very subjective, all-too-human side of religion—it dealt neither with God, with doctrine, nor with the nature of the redemptive community. It did not even deal with the nature of faith. To be sure, it touched upon the nature of man, but only so lightly and so humanly that it necessitated no change in churchmen's thoughts about God and his relation to man. Moreover, even James's pragmatism was sufficiently palatable to the prevailing theological climate of the time to prevent all too vigorous skirmishes.

My thesis is that James set up narrow boundaries to the field of the psychology of religion and that many of his successors held to those limits without giving the matter much thought. Perhaps they found the limitation tactically useful. Some exceptions must be noted, but they had little influence. The Wiemans (1935), for instance, deplored the fact. A few of James's contemporaries, notably Coe (1916) and Leuba (1912), were more daring on this point, but most students take no recourse to their original works. Leuba must be credited with having faced the question of the existence and the nature of God; he took the viewpoint that religion deals with an illusory reality. Freud would have more to say about that later.

Religious life involves images, intuitions, concepts, and the human history of all these about God. But, above all, it involves an object relation with God, and psychology must be interested in all these aspects. I am not sure whether psychology can or should waive the ontological question, as, by the way, some theological systems also do, but I am sure that it cannot stop short of man's thinking about God and the forming and obtaining of his image. Beside the feelingful renditions of religious feelings stand the thoughtful renditions of religious thinking. Diary pages, such as James used, may be excellent sources to get at feelings; it would seem to me that theological treatises are the appropriate sources for religious thoughts in an articulate form. Psychology is interested in what psychoanalysts call the primary as well as the secondary processes of religion, in the latent dream thoughts as well as in the dream work and the manifest dream content, including the secondary elaborations.

The method of the James tradition consists chiefly, if not exclusively, in non-experimental fact finding and description. Use is made of biographical materials, questionnaires, and simple or complex (but mostly simple) cor-

101

relation techniques. Much work has gone into correlating incidence of conversion, frequency of prayer, loyalty to parental beliefs, etc., with global personality traits.

There were others of course. An interesting psychologist of religion is R. Mueller-Freienfels (1920), who published two little volumes in German. His work is broad and helpfully systematic but not always deep. Of particular importance is his description of the field: individual forms and institutional forms of religion are put side by side, and much attention is paid to myths, liturgy, and such religious acts as prayer and sacrifice. He uses no special methods of investigation but works, as many students of religion do, from his desk, using a simple Kantian scheme which emphasizes feeling, willing, and thinking. Under "thinking" are included all possible cognitive aspects of religion: the acquisition of knowledge, contemplation, the exercise of logical functions, and the use of symbols. I believe that this latter emphasis is of importance.

Mueller-Freienfels' contribution also contains a helpful schematization of historical trends in the psychology of religion. He considers the following six tendencies or schools of thought:

1. Theological schools of thought which try to give psychological underpinnings for a given theological system. An example is Schleiermacher, who defined religion in its subjective aspects as the feeling of utter dependence.
2. The ethnopsychological school produced by French and English positivism, exemplified in Wundt's work.
3. A school of differential psychology particularly strong in America, with its traditional interest in individual differences. Examples: Leuba, James, Starbuck.
4. A psychopathological school, particularly strong in France. Examples: Delacroix, Flournoy.
5. An analytic school aiming at an independent analysis of traditional religion, knowing that its psychological roots are often purposely hidden from scrutiny. Examples: Feuerbach and perhaps Nietzsche.
6. The psychoanalytic school, which emphasizes the role of unconscious motivation, of drives, and of the function of the superego.

We will come back to some of these schools later and consider psychoanalysis first.

Psychoanalytic studies of religion started early in this century. One of Freud's first case studies, that of the wolf man (Freud, 1918), contained some interesting notes on the role of religion in psychopathology. In addition to Freud's *Totem and Taboo* (1913) and *The Future of an Illusion* (1928), the works of Pfister (1923, 1944) and of Jones (1951, 1951a, 1951b) must be mentioned here. Because of the general hostility to psychoanalysis in the early decades of our century there was at first very little carry-over of the analysts' observations and theories into the main body of religious studies. Why it failed to be taken seriously by the official body of the psychology of religion is a more complex riddle. A 1958 textbook (Clark, 1958), under the somewhat presumptuous title *"The" Psychology of Religion,* contents itself with some meaningless eulogies on Freud but fails to make use of the main propositions of psychoanalysis. Even the work of Pfister, the Swiss pastor and one of Freud's earliest and most sincere colleagues, is not mentioned.

Psychoanalytic studies of religion have, of course, a special character, conceptually as well as methodologically. They are basically studies of motivation for religion, and the person's set of beliefs and practices are approached from the point of view of wish fulfilment, drive control, primary and secondary-process thinking, object relations, the genesis of conscience and the ego ideal, and the economics of libidinal and aggressive urges. Because the word "symptom" in psychoanalysis covers an almost infinite range of possibilities, religion can be approached as a symptom. Psychoanalysis said more forcefully what James had said earlier, namely, that people *use* their God.

The mechanics of the psychic household, the defense processes of the ego, and the fundamental psychosocial constellations, such as the oedipal conflict, were all brought to bear upon religion, phylogenetically as well as ontogenetically, individually and collectively, within a genetic-dynamic formula. This formula added an entirely new dimension to the methodology of the psychology of religion in that it demanded longitudinal assessment of the individual in the network of his object relationships. It also holds that personal documents, which were the mainstay of James's studies, cannot be taken at face value but must be approached with analytic sophistication. And, since for practical reasons such studies nearly always coincide with the process of psychotherapy, an excellent opportunity is here provided for evaluating the significance of religion in relation to other pursuits, preoccupations, values, and needs of the individual. In other words, here is one place where one can study how religion "fits" into life.

An interesting feature of psychoanalytic study of religion is its shortening of the psychological distance between God and man. Note that I speak here of psychological, not of ontological, distance. God's names, as Jones has remarked, such as Father, Maker, Sustainer, and Provider, are relevant to the family drama. To me, the statement that God is a father figure may also imply its complement—that biological fathers have numinous qualities. In other words, psychoanalysis has established a new affinity (not identity) between God and man which cuts across the technical distinction between God's transcendence and his immanence.

As to the old dispute on psychology's relation to the ontological question about God, I would like to make a second comment. It seems to me a perfectly psychological question to ask why and on what grounds some people answer the ontological question about God vigorously in the affirmative, why some deny it, and why a third group of people say that they do not know. Particularly since the matter cannot be decided logically, as even some theologians admit, the psychology of knowledge, like the sociology of knowledge, may have some important contributions to make. The ontological question with capital letters is one thing; but every individual's way of coming to grips with it is quite a different thing.

Freud's term "illusion," denoting the formal psychological status of religious belief, has given rise to bitter opposition, particularly from those who have only read the title of his book. The book itself (Freud, 1928) clarifies the meaning of the term: religious beliefs are illusions in the sense that they are not pure products of experience or end results of thinking but fulfilments of the oldest, strongest, and most urgent wishes of mankind. An illusion is not a mistake. Rather it is like Columbus thinking he had discovered a new seaway to India, while he had actually discovered America! An illusion is not necessarily false, that is, incapable of realization or contradictory to reality. The great question is: If illusions are needed, how we can have those that are capable of correction; how we can have those that will not deteriorate into delusions?

I can find little fault with these definitions. They bring to my mind Paul's admonition to the Corinthians: "For now we see in a mirror dimly, but then we will see face to face." Knowledge of God is always approximate and always full of distortions; it needs correction at any stage in life. Of this, the sincere Christian should be more convinced than anyone else. Our psychic organization, our perceptions, our thoughts, our wishes, our moods participate in the shaping of our beliefs. We knew this before the "New Look" in perception and before the concept of perceptual defense. As the theologian Tillich (1957) points out, our doubts codetermine the dynamics of our faith. The divine purpose is never completely known by mortals, and, because of this, we find ourselves making guesses about it. The guesses may not be unaided; they may be wise and inspired; but they remain *our* guesses. Moreover, as Jones has remarked, "what one wants to know about the divine purpose is its intention towards oneself" (Jones, 1951). It is exactly because religion deals not with abstractions but with realities by which to live that psychoanalytic formulations must be taken seriously.

But perhaps the most significant contribution of psychoanalysis to the psychology of religion is its insistence upon the role of conflict in religion, and of religion in conflict, personal as well as social. Religion is now no longer an item or parcel of experience but a quality of an individual's experiencing the world and himself; it can be defined as a way of problem-solving. This point had already been made in 1911 by a non-analytic psychologist, George M. Stratton (1911), who saw the source of religion in man's being entangled in all kind of conflicts, stemming from inner and outer polarities. I believe that this position is heuristically of great importance to the psychology of religion. Several questions come to mind right away:

1. Which problems have been solved or can be solved by religion?
2. What kind of religion can solve a given problem?
3. To what extent are problems really solved by religion or which problems are refractory to religious solutions?
4. Can a man fall back on traditional religious thoughts and beliefs, or must he look for religious innovations?
5. Which new problems are in turn posed by attempts at problem-solving through religion?
6. Does religion, as it is used in problem-solving, remain itself problem-free or does it become conflict-laden?

Some of these latter questions seem particularly relevant to certain developments within Protestant theology and to recent thinking on the problem of mental health. Both Christianity and mental health seem to require some degree of tension and of "considered non-conformity" (Shoben, 1957), to use Shoben's beautiful phrase.

At any rate, within such a framework the concept of religious experience as a state has to give way to the concept of religion as a process. Problem-solving takes time, and it always involves a future, that is, the unknown. Phenomenologically, it may even mean a preoccupation with the unknown (Polanyi, 1957; Pruyser, 1959). The person who is engaged in problem-solving proceeds by hypotheses—one after another. How are his hypotheses corrected under the impact of experience? How does he draw, and modify, his cognitive maps?

With psychoanalysis the psychology of religion should have undergone a change in concepts, in orientation, and in attitude toward the material studied. Instead, it underwent a change in personnel. For psychoanalysis is also a branch of psychiatry and, through it, of medicine. Within psychology, its impact was felt mostly in the specialization of clinical psychology, which has had relatively little contact with the psychology of religion—the latter has remained more closely in the fold of academic psychology and educational psychology. The psychoanalytic impact on psychiatry is great. Its impact is also felt keenly in pastoral education, even in pastoral theology. I believe that this selective spread of the influence of psychoanalysis is altering the status of scientific concern with religion in a major way.

First of all, it has meant a shift from pure science to applied science. Second, it has meant a shift from the traditional academic department to the professional training program. Third, much, if not most, of the activity in

105

psychology and religion has moved from the university campus to the psychiatric clinic, the hospital, and the parish. Indeed, the combination "religion and psychiatry" is now more popular than the psychology of religion, and pastoral theology is rapidly becoming also a pastoral psychology.

Many of these changes seem to depend on the emergence of a new professional specialty, that of the psychotherapist, and on the uncertainty about the prerequisites for his training. But whoever he may be, and whatever his academic background, it is important to note for our purposes that his role implies both a marvelous opportunity and a profounl ambiguity in relation to the possibility of an advancing psychology of religion. The psychotherapist admittedly combines science and art, and he combines them in unsteady proportions. On the one hand, he is in a unique position of nearness to deep and subtle processes, just at that level of depth which many of us have surmised is the level at which religion may be significant in a person's life. Certainly, he reaches a stratum of personality functioning by which the psychology of religion could be immensely enriched. But the deeper he goes with his patient, the more difficult it becomes for him to maintain the cool, objective, and detached attitude of the curious scientist. Moreover, the psychotherapist's endeavor to help (and "helping" is one of the foremost definitions of his profession) is matched by his patient's desire to obtain health, and this may place the observational data about the patient's religion, if any, in a distorted, or at least very limited, perspective. For, despite the intriguingly deep level at which observations about an individual's religion may be obtained in such a setting, the purpose of "helping" and "being helped" tends to give rise to cheap superficialities about religion as a mode of, a vehicle for, or a critierion of adjustment or to the tedious attempts at establishing correlations or even equations between religion and mental health.

This perhaps is as good a place as any to mention the works of Jung, though it is nearly impossible to do justice in a few paragraphs to this penetrating and rich thinker. Since his extensive writings cover many borderland areas among psychology, psychiatry, medicine, history of religion, theology, and cultural anthropology (Jung, 1933, 1938, 1952, 1954), it would be tempting to confine ourselves here to Jung's contribution to the psychology of religion proper. However, his own demonstration of the interweaving among so many diverse themes, constructs, observations, and symbols makes such a restriction intolerable. They are all relevant to the psychology of religion, though some more peripherally than others.

One will search in vain for the classical chapter headings of psychology of religion in Jung's works. There are no systematic treatises on the religion of adolescence or on conversion. There is very little material on individual differences in religion. All these and many other topics are scattered throughout his works, sometimes in relation to religion, sometimes in connection with non-religious aspects of living. But there is an abundance of rich, searching, and sometimes daring propositions from which the psychology of religion could greatly benefit.

While several thinkers have stated that people *use* their gods, there is probably no one who has come so close as Jung has to saying that people also *make* their gods. Lest one be frightened or repelled by the implications of this position, it should be noted that Jung is one contemporary psychologist who does not shrink away from the "soul," which he at times even seems to prefer to the more neutral and technical term "psyche." Added to this is his conception of human life as a process of individuation in which the self and its destiny are actively sought and nurtured. The journey of the self is described as a road toward salvation—indeed, the soul and the self (though objects of empirical study) have by postulate been given a sacramental and pseudo-divine status! Hence Jung is able, from this position, to study the psychological side of the whole process in which man lives with his God and God with "his" men, in terms of the religio-psychological border-line concept of "archetypes."

God is here no longer an abstraction, no mere "Prime Mover" or "Summum Bonum," but something to which people feel related *in tension* (Hofmann, 1955). In other words, psychology of religion can be a psychology of interaction and interpersonal relationships with supernatural beings in which not only man but also God and the dialogue between them become objects of analysis. For God is not the projection of a thought or idea onto another person (as the paranoic patient may project some quality of himself onto someone else), but he is projected *as a person*. Thus he is within reach of personality theory. In his *Answer to Job* Jung is indeed consequent enough to describe God as a changing, developing Being who learns to respond to one man's exemplary morality. He also discusses the difficult problem of God's sexual identity.

No doubt there are reasons to worry about the solidity of Jung's premises and conclusions, but nevertheless it remains true that his propositions "will stand as a watershed between the traditional and the coming psychology of religion," as Hofmann (1955) has said.

But psychotherapy is only one era in which the hand of dynamic psychology and psychiatry is shown. There is another, and perhaps much wider, field of professional endeavor in healing relevant to the psychology of religion. That is the field of hospital psychiatry. I think that the development of modern hospital psychiatry, as distinct from mere custodial care, has also some important implications for the psychology of religion. I will take these up under two headings: the composite of professional specialties on the psychiatric team and the nature of psychiatric case study.

First, the modern psychiatric team shows division of labor and specialization of functioning with the preservation of a common goal—healing. But the division of labor is not complete; there is indeed much overlap between the functions of the team members and considerable unity in basic scientific theory. Psychiatrist, psychologist, social worker, and chaplain, to mention only a few team members, all work together in the evaluation and the treatment of the patient under the integrating aegis of the psychiatrist. The modern mental hospital is also, more than it ever was, a social institution which maintains many intimate ties with the community. It interacts, more or less intensely, with many professional and social groups: local physicians, judges, ministers and priests, civic groups, welfare agencies, and various religious organizations such as churches and councils of churches. Many different persons and forces are marshaled on behalf of "total care" for the patient. Some of these groups or individuals have an obvious and direct concern with the religious welfare of the hospitalized patient before, during, and after his temporary isolation. Much of this activity has become channelized and epitomized in a new professional specialty—the mental-hospital chaplain. And this is the place to highlight one more chapter in the history of the psychology of religion written by Anton Boisen.

In his profound book, *The Exploration of the Inner World,* Boisen (1936) put a new stamp on psychopathology and religion by placing both in the framework of the life-crisis. Religious experience can best be understood if it is seen in the same order of intensity and depth that attaches to severe mental illness. Both are processes of disorganization and reorganization of personality, of transformation, dealing with man's potentialities and ultimate loyalties. I think that this is a position which places religious experience functionally and experientially most clearly at the nexus of holistic, integrating tendencies of the organism. In this theoretical framework religion is not an adjuvant to integration; it is integration. It is one way of solving problems, sometimes successfully. Religion and mental illness, and of course by implication also mental health, are to be approached as existential conditions. Specific categories of experience obtain the focus in mental illness and in religion: world catastrophe, death and rebirth, the feeling of cosmic importance and of personal responsibility and mission. Religious language is close to the "primary-process" language known from psychoanalysis.

Whatever one may think of Boisen's propositions in detail, they certainly stress a dimension that is much needed in the psychology of religion. The mental-hospital chaplain with special clinical-pastoral training as a part of the psychiatric team is chiefly Boisen's creation. His is a unique function: he represents religion in all its aspects on the psychiatric team and to the patients. We must ask what implications this has for the psychology of religion.

The chaplain is first of all a pastor, not a theologian. His task lies in shepherding, co-ordinate with the healing goal of the psychiatric team, which goal he shares. But he is the only member of the team whose contact with the patients is voluntary—he cannot be made part of a therapeutic regime even if this would involve clear benefits toward the patient's healing. For our purposes the most significant part of his function is that it brings him into contact with persons who have met with utter failure in problem-solving, with or without religion or pseudo-religion, and at times with failure in earlier attempts at religious problem-solving, which has resulted in specific resistances to even the faintest religious allusions. If Boisen's thesis is correct, the chaplain is forced to *seek* religion in psychopathology; and he finds it— sometimes in obvious manifestations of psychopathology *of* religion, some- times in seemingly non-religious processes, and at other times nowhere. I believe that this has some major consequences. While James and the tradi- tional body of the psychology of religion focused on the more obviously and indisputably religious experience—on the "pure cases," so to speak— the chaplain is, as all ministers of the faith are, broadening the range of religious data immensely by including all potentially religious phenomena. The old question was: Which are the significant data of religious experi- ence? The new question is: Which data of experience are of religious significance?

Now let us look at the clinical psychologist on the psychiatric team. Can he assess and evaluate the religious experience of his patients, if any? My personal experience as a member of such a team has been enigmatic, perhaps even shocking. I have been intrigued by the absence of spontaneous religious references in test responses and interviews, even among ardent churchgoers. Some of our tests seem able to tap fairly deep levels of personality function- ing, and yet we rarely encounter a clearly religious response to our Rorschach and Thematic Apperception tests. Patients say many things and sometimes indulge in a large amount of moralizing; they may even see a church steeple in an inkblot, but this appears on further scrutiny to be purely an architectural or a scenic-idyllic item. Where in the tests do we find their religion? Is it a failure of our tests, or is it proof of the negligible role of religion in the life of many people, admitting that we actually deal with a selected group? Or is it perhaps the result of the patient's social perception which compartmentalizes all encounters with people in terms of specific roles? Does the patient seek out the chaplain to talk about religion, only to ignore this dimension of his life in his meeting with other team members? I do not know the full answer to these questions, but I surmise that they can all be answered with a partial "Yes."

For the psychology of religion this situation means that the clinical psychologist will not readily be able to furnish new data. As a matter of fact, the first datum is negative: there is not as much religion as we might have thought.

But here again we have to heed the question: Which data of experience are of religious significance? Could it be that the patients are giving us religious responses without our knowing it? And perhaps without their own conscious knowledge? There was a time when sexual references in language, action, and fantasy went by unrecognized, because the power of sex and the role of symbolism were not understood. At that time sex was, by the civilized, delegated to a separate and remote chamber of the mind or, rather, the body. Perhaps we are in the psychology of religion in the same stage at which sexology was in the days of Havelock Ellis and Krafft-Ebbing.

A second comment about psychologists may be in order. In several of my colleagues who are articulate, introspective, and sensitive people and who subscribe to an integrated set of religious propositions, the reading of standard texts on the psychology of religion elicits disappointment. I have always shared their reaction; we sense keenly that the heart of the matter has not been reached. In the same vein there is even among some writers of these books a hardly hidden overtone of hopelessness with regard to the relevance of their own works. Does it mean that they feel psychology is still too young to tackle such a formidable task? Or must we think of the possible role of repression which handicaps even psychologists in coming to grips with religion? Perhaps we can learn something from that mighty pre-scientific psychologist Feuerbach (1957), who put all his emphasis on the given existence, that is, the sensing, thinking, and self-actualizing persons, and who had the temerity to say, "Theology is anthropology," because in the object of religion nothing but the essence of man is expressed. Of course, Feuerbach's "nothing but" is dogmatic and to that extent unscientific, but his temerity, rigor, ardor, and immense curiosity are to be envied this day.

The effectiveness of hospital psychiatry depends in very large measure on the adequacy of the case study. What is psychiatric case study? Several books have been written on the subject (Masserman, 1955; Menninger, 1952), but the essence of it lies in what psychiatrists do, which is, according to Menninger, "try to understand their patients." The case study is a formulation of that understanding. It is written purposefully, with the double aim of communicating the understanding to others and of marshaling all the available forces and knowledge to change the patient's condition. A good case study usually involves all the specialists on the team, but first of all it requires the observational powers, the analytic acumen, the persistence in pursuing significant detail, the search for meaning, and, above all, the synthesizing ability of the psychiatrist. Our question is: How can a psychiatric case study be made relevant to the psychology of religion? Note that I do not speak here of *psychopathology* of religion, although it is

110

likely that, in a patient population, religion may be part of the presenting symptoms. I am assuming that mental illness need not engulf the whole person—in other words, that religion may be an area of healthy functioning in a person quite aberrant in other spheres or aspects of life.

A good many psychiatric case studies begin with phrases like this: "This is the case of a white, thirty-five-year-old, prim, Methodist, midwestern housewife," only to omit any further reference to the religious dimension in this person's life, except perhaps for a note on the role that the choir or the Sunday school played in getting her acquainted with her husband. Meanwhile the phrase itself is a perfect stereotype and sets up all kinds of expectancies which may help channelize possible interpretations. On the other hand, some books on the psychology of religion make use of the case-study method (as, e.g., Johnson, 1957, 1959, does quite effectively) only to emphasize all possible aspects of experience relevant to religion, but with a neglect of the person's sexual history, his infantile and childhood experiences, his economic history, etc. I think that in both instances the psychology of religion does not really profit from the clinical case-study method, and this judgment stems from my ardent belief that it could profit so much if the case study were done with care, holistically, existentially, and following the natural articulations of the patient's subjective and objective reality. Nor should my allusion to the phrase "prim, Methodist housewife" be taken as a persiflage of the writing of case studies. I admit—nay, I am even proposing—that the psychiatric assessment of the religious dimension in the life of a patient is an extremely difficult business. And let me add that it is very difficult for the patient's pastor too.

But we must make an attempt, and our procedures must be fair to the reality which we want to assess. We need not assume that everyone is deeply religious, but neither may we assume that religion is a compartmentalized area of a patient's life and, consequently, delegate its assessment to the chaplain or some other specialist or simply ignore it. To be sure, in some people religion *is* compartmentalized, but that is psychologically an interesting phenomenon which merits special mention and interpretation. Above all, it seems to me that we can in no case expect "religious data" just to pop up. Strictly speaking, there are no religious data, ready to take, just as little as there are any sexual data. Rather *all* data—events, processes, actions, objects, and object relations—may have either or both a religious and sexual significance for the patient, or for the examiner, or for both.

There is still a different angle on this problem. Even in well-documented and well-integrated psychiatric case studies religious references are often missing. Sometimes this may be because of the examiner's lack of interest, but sometimes it happens despite attempts at obtaining religious relevancies from the patient. I cannot quite explain this, except that I have a hunch that the faith of many people may be completely inarticulate, and in others

111

it may rarely reach a level where explicit references to it can be made. I also surmise that in some patients, and perhaps in many normal people, specific religious qualities and numinous values have shifted from traditional and suitable objects to what theologians would call idolatrous objects, concerns, pursuits, and values (Cherbonnier, 1955). The chromium-plated car with the juke-box rear, the life-style of suburbia, the pursuit of confirmism, the aspiration to orgastic potency, and the zealous search for mental health are cases in point. If there is some validity in this speculation, the psychology of religion may be greatly enhanced and enriched by a meticulous study of people's idols and idolatries. The scientific study of religion must include *all* gods, *all* numina, all ultimate concerns, even those that may turn out to be false ultimates. I know of no better way to accomplish this than by a thorough application of the clinical method in psychiatric case study—a method which attempts to portray and conceptualize "what men live by." Why not assess, as part of the case study, what a person considers holy?

If we are indeed concerned with all gods, we must also deal with *all* the ways of man in worship, prayer, and ritual. Books on the psychology of religion have usually emphasized the diversity of styles and types of such religious actions. But there is a conspicuous limitation of approach in relation to prayer. Entirely typical is the following statement which I found in the 1958 textbook to which I have already alluded: "In studying prayer we have the additional difficulty of surveying an area of the inner life of which the average person is loath to speak. If one prays at all, the matter is apt to concern his very dearest wishes." The conclusion drawn from this observation is that the psychologist's curiosity should therefore be tempered by his reverence; in regard to prayer, he must content himself with "soft techniques" such as questionnaires and gentle interviews.

I am entirely at odds with such a policy. Prayer has been widely considered as "the heart of religion." The phenomenologist Heiler (1932) has said that it is the most spontaneous and the most personal expression of religion. If this is so, the psychology of religion must look for ways of coming to grips with it. And again I believe that the psychiatrist and clinical psychologist are here in a unique position to contribute, because of their rich knowledge of, and total concern for, their charges. Meanwhile, the psychologist of religion can learn another lesson from the history of psychoanalysis: if observations on others are difficult to make, he can observe himself. Freud (1953) analyzed his own dreams and published them in order to advance the science of dream interpretation. I would invite the religious ones among the curious scientists of religion to study their own prayers, including just these "dearest wishes" about which the "average person is loath to speak." Science knows no taboos, and *noblesse oblige*.

So far, I have stayed within the framework of the psychology of religion in the formal professional sense. I mentioned psychiatry and the mental-

112

hospital chaplaincy only in terms of how they contribute to the process of assessing and evaluating the role of religion in life, the nature of an individual's faith, and the possible distortions thereof. The aims of psychiatry, and particularly of the chaplaincy, do not coincide with the aims of psychology. This review cannot be brought to a conclusion without considering at least one more discipline, the aims of which are widely different from those of psychology, but from whose matrix of observations, theories, and speculations exceedingly important contributions to the psychology of religion have been made. That discipline is theology, or the body of divinity.

We cannot go into the problem of how this vast body is internally articulated and how it relates to the arts and sciences. (In his recent book on pastoral theology, Hiltner [1958] offers an interesting schema of these relations.) Nor can I venture here to review all the psychological relevancies of theological studies, although I am convinced that there are many. This would be beyond the scope of this presentation and perhaps beyond my competence. I say "perhaps" because I feel that it would take a *psychologist* to establish such psychological relevancies, but I also realize that this is a formidable task. Systematic theology usually contains more or less elaborate doctrines of man; moral theology presents values and goals for human behavior and includes admonitions and adhortations; pastoral theology presents aims and methods of shepherding. In all these there is at least an implied psychology, dealing with the actual and the ideal conditions of man, with origins, alienation, motives, values, conscience, goals, conflict, repair, and learning. It would take us too far afield to examine here any of these psychological implications of theology, but I think that it can and should be done for the advancement of the psychology of religion.

Some theologians have been quite explicit on psychological matters. While Schleiermacher (1928) formulated his thesis on faith as the feeling of "utter dependency," still with a clearly apologetic aim, for some later theologians apologetics has given way to precise description and analysis of psychic states in faith for its own sake. Two of them, Otto and Tillich, must be mentioned here because of their immense value to the psychology of religion.

Otto's (1923, 1957) celebrated phenomenological study *The Idea of the Holy* and his later work *Mysticism East and West* have left a deep impression on readers in many different professions. His two-pronged approach to the subjective and objective pole of the core experience in religion, that is, the idea of the holy or numinous corresponding in each of its aspects with specific moments of human experience, is a masterpiece of methodology. The emphasis is not on individual differences, although some striking differences are portrayed, but on the "common good" of religion, on the generalities that govern religious experience. But experience is related at every step with its object; the science of man as *Homo religiosus* and the science of God are not divorced. Otto's phenomenological analysis is a convincing answer to the fallacious assumption that the psychology of religion deals only with man—it must deal with God, for religion is the establishing, experiencing, and nurturing of a relation between God and man. There is no psychology of the artist apart from the artistic work and beauty that is given form, neither can there be a psychology of religion apart from the idea of God and the forms in which holiness becomes transparent. Just as theology deals also with man, psychology must deal also with the numinous.

And this is my reason for having quoted Allport's searching statement and for thinking that psychology of religion cannot, out of fear of the ontological question, avoid all references to God. Psychology cannot be theology or philosophy, but neither can it behave like the ostrich with its peculiar technique for shutting out fearsome objects. The truth of a religious assertion is a substantial part of the religious experience, for *Homo religiosus* is passionately involved in it and ultimately concerned with it. When a truth turns out to be disappointing, when it lets us down, we must reorganize our lives and seek a better truth; else we become ill. Whether God-in-general is real or not, the God-in-particular of this or that believer must be at least realistic. Not sensually or concretistically, in that "He walks with me and He talks with me" (this is Whitehead's "fallacy of misplaced concreteness"; or what Woodger labels the "finger and thumb philosophy"); neither as a loose thought or even as a concept, but in the psychological sense that God is loved and responded to by people who live with him. Frued's definition, "illusion," with specifications that I mentioned, is not such a bad term after all.

A psychology of religion without some evaluation of God is a narrow undertaking. Though it is true that the reality of God cannot be asserted or denied by psychology, it is also true that a deliberately agnostic attitude on the part of the scientist cannot do full justice to the nature of the experience of God in believing subjects. I would hold that a humorless scientist cannot write a full psychology of humor; not can the dreamless psychologist ever write the rich scientific text of dreams that Freud wrote. To know what aspects of experience have religious significance for a person presupposes some familiarity with the possibilities and perplexities of religion in the investigator.

I think, then, that the psychology of religion may assume an attitude of naïve realism toward the object of religious beliefs. All sciences take this attitude toward their direct and indirect objects. The philosophical critique of this position is a matter for the philosophy of science, not for the sciences themselves. To assume this attitude is not to place psychology in the service of religious apologetics. If, as Whitehead (1925) holds, religion is one of the strong forces which influence man, and if the believers place one source of this force in God, the psychologist must study Gods *for the sake of studying man*. I use the plural form here to indicate, moreover, that what is relevant to the believer is God's attributes in relation to himself rather than the general idea of God. And these are exactly some items of difference between various theologies. In some way, the problem of God's existence is to be approached as an individualized and particular, rather than a general, question. Woodger (1956) has remarked that it is difficult to distinguish existing from existing for *someone*. Its parallel in the psychology of religion is that God is never a simple object, one among many, but always a *love* object to the devout person. Now *love* objects have a plus factor to the lover which outsiders cannot observe. To me, my spouse has attributes which my neighbors will never perceive. That is why my relationship with her is more dynamic than my neighbors'; it involves commitment, loyalty, exaltation, and a highly particularized order of reality. Again, Woodger states that it is impossible to know that something exists without knowing something else about it.

Existentially oriented thinkers have had far less trouble with the ontological problem than the classical theologians. They have seen that the arguments for God's existence are less relevant to religious vitality and truth than had been assumed. They have seen the profound but sublime irrationality of all religious propositions. They have noticed, moreover, that God-centeredness is not necessarily the opposite of man-centeredness. The various Cartesian splits between being and knowing, subject and object, natural and spiritual realms, are only some possible options of human thought. It is unscientific to take them as dogma. Hebrew genius produced another possibility, namely, that the knowledge of man and the knowledge of God are covariants. To the extent that some religious men proceed on this premise, the psychology of religion may accept it as a postulate and knowingly assume the implied ontological position. I do not think that it will stop being a science for that matter.

Much affinity with the existential mode of thought is present in the works of Tillich (1952, 1957). In *The Courage to Be* and *Dynamics of Faith* he stands in part on the shoulders of Otto. His expressions, "ultimate concern" and "centered act of the personality," have a strong appeal to dynamic psychologists, for they reach the motivational depths, the urge character, the directional qualities, and the forever-conflict-laden ways of human problem-solving. Tillich's emphasis on the cognitive process in religion, epitomized in his definition of faith as including the dynamics of doubt, offers much to the psychology of religion. Religion can now be seen as exploratory behavior, driven, among other things, by man's curiosity and by his perpetual attempts to maximize contact with a maximal environment to the full deployment of all his potentialities. The psychology of learning is interested in such propositions. Tillich's specifications of anxiety, and his emphasis on the dynamics of courage, have aroused considerable interest in psychological and psychiatric circles. I believe that the pursuit of just these subtle psychological processes implied in the terms "faith," "courage," "doubt," "concern"—and I would like to add "hope" (Marcel, 1944) and "love" (Menniger, 1942)—will, in the long run, provide exactly the enrichment of the psychology of religion that our science is waiting for. Our science is a sober but not inhibited, an imaginative but not fantastic, concern. The psychology of religion must be attuned to the double goal of using disciplined thought and of keeping religion in the equation.

Humanistic Religious Psychology

Orlo Strunk, Jr.

Despite arid times and periods of near eclipse, the psychology of religion has manifested a fascinating and strangely persistent style of survival. When William James elected to speak on what he called "man's religious constitution" as his Gifford Lectures at the University of Edinburgh in 1900, he could not have guessed that his subject matter would launch a discipline capable of attracting some of the keenest minds in Europe and America. Even recognizing the fact that there were several eminent scholars in the field before James's excursion—he himself acknowledged some of them in the Preface to *The Varieties of Religious Experience* (James, 1902)—it was undoubtedly James who set the stage and established part of the future pattern of the discipline. More important still, it was James who promoted the humanistic spirit which has tended to reassert itself whenever the field has been in danger of annihilation via insipid scientism.

HISTORIC ASPECTS OF RELIGIOUS PSYCHOLOGY

Though this is not the place to offer a history of the psychology of religion—a feat not yet consummated by any contemporary scholar—an historic sensitivity of a sort is needed if one is to see how contemporary humanistic psychology is both an innovational propulsion for the psychology

From *The Journal of Pastoral Care*, 24 (1970), 90-97.

of religion and at the same time a catalytic reminder to the discipline of some of its original intentions as established by its founder, William James.

When psychological science first glimpsed the possibility that religion, as the British anthropologist Sir James Frazer put it, could be approached "as phenomena of consciousness to be studied like any other aspect of human nature" (Frazer, 1927) an idea and a principle came forth which would mold a new discipline, potentially second only in boldness to Freudian psychoanalysis, which from its inception did not hesitate to examine religions and religious behavior. And like psychoanalysis, the psychology of religion's reception into the halls of the behavioral sciences was stormy, partial, and highly complex.

In the United States, where behaviorism already was beginning to get a throat hold on the psychological profession, the psychology of religion could be entertained only by a handful of eminent psychologists—G. Stanley Hall (1904), James H. Leuba (1912), E. D. Starbuck (1903), and, of course, William James (1902).

Hall was able to promote the field under the authority of not only his stature as the founder and first president of the American Psychological Association, but because he was also the chief administrative officer of an American university. Besides, he was not the kind of man to have an interest thwarted by the snifflings of scientific purists. Undoubtedly his personal interest in the field motivated him to pursue it with some vigor, although he himself recognized that his professional life was "a series of fads or crazes," and his interest in the psychology of religion was but one of many such excursions.

The case was different with James H. Leuba, who brought to the field an empirical zeal comparable to any contemporary behaviorist. Hiltner's evaluation of Leuba's contributions now appears a bit severe: ". . . unlike James, his general attitude to religion has been anti rather than pro. Indeed, Leuba was the earliest and most obvious reductionist among the psychologists of religion. Because of his scholarship, his works had to be taken seriously. But no one liked them except those whose attitudes also demanded a dethronement of all gods. Since this was the clear, and eventually the stated, purpose of Leuba's work, it is doubtful how much he may be considered interested in a psychological *understanding* of religion" (Hiltner, 1947). Despite Leuba's intentions, he represents another of the pioneers whose approach was severely conditioned by the *Zeitgeist,* in this instance reductionism.

E. D. Starbuck, on the other hand, felt the same pressures from all his colleagues as did Leuba, but he approached the phenomena with sympathy and insisted that the psychological study of religion was as legitimate a topic for psychologists as any other. The exact contributions of Starbuck have not yet been fully identified and appreciated, but there are reasons to believe that he was the first psychologist to use the term "psychology of religion," and this over the objections of his psychological colleagues who at the time felt that such an association could only lead to no good end.

In a real sense, these early pioneers stuck their intellectual necks out by expressing interest in religion. They became fair game for psychologists and theologians alike. But there was no stopping the interest that had been uncovered by these early works, and in the early nineteen hundreds a moderately impressive line of psychologists and theologians began to do research and to write books. The movement took a firm hold in New England—especially at Boston University under the leadership of F. L. Strickland (1924) and later Paul E. Johnson (1945; 1959); and it found further extensions on the other side of the Charles River in the text by Walter H. Clark (1958) at Andover Newton Theological School, and the important excursion at Harvard University of Gordon W. Allport (1950).

Since James, literally thousands of books and articles have appeared which legitimately might fall under the rubric "psychology of religion." One of the most recent bibliographies identifies nearly six thousand items in social scientific studies of religion (Berkowitz & Johnson, 1967), many directly oriented in terms of traditional religious psychology. Add to this the excellent annotated bibliography of W. W. Meissner (1961), with its nearly three thousand items, and we see that the psychology of religion has produced a relatively impressive body of literature. Even acknowledging the fact that the applied areas of pastoral counseling and religion and mental health have greatly overshadowed the field, empirical and religio-psychological research in the area of religious phenomena continues at a rapid pace. Two very recent volumes, Joseph Havens' *Psychology and Religion* (1968) and Paul W. Pruyser's *A Dynamic Psychology of Religion* (1968), demonstrate the current interests, the latter presenting approaches to religious behavior and experience consistent with much in contemporary clinical psychology and at the tame time in keeping with the humanistic spirit of James.

RESISTANCE TO PSYCHOLOGY OF RELIGION

But throughout this somewhat fascinating development there has been a strange dynamic at work. André Godin has aptly characterized it as "eagerness for and resistance to the scientific psychology of religion" (Godin, 1964). Within organized religion there has been a vigorous interest in psychological insights and what they might reveal as to the nature of the religious sentiment. At the same time, there has been a cautious resistance to the field, especially to that type of "nothing but" psychology which tended to blanket the American scene during the behavioristic eclipse. And within psychology proper there has been an eagerness on the part of a surprising number of psychologists to study religion, especially by those comprehensive theorists who were convinced that psychology, if it is to be anything worthwhile, cannot neglect any aspect of man's behavior and experience. At the same time, psychology has resisted concerted attempts to treat the religious sentiment intensely and seriously, feeling, as Starbuck's colleagues did at the turn of the century, that such an association might taint the objective purity so cherished by much of the psychological community.

These historic and contemporary propensities are illustrated remarkably well in the phrase "psychology of religion" as contrasted with the term "religious psychology." In Germany the term *Religionspsychologie* is used extensively to describe the field known in America as the psychology of religion. Americans invariably and rightly translate the term *Religionspsychologie* as "psychology of religion," but their reason is not simply a linguistic predilection; the phrase "psychology of religion" suggests an objective commitment lost in the term "religious psychology," which seems to imply a religious stance of the psychologist. It is an interesting but telling artifact that we do not assume an industrial psychologist to be necessarily an industrialist or that a child psychologist is a child, but we are prone to think that a religious psychologist must surely be religious!

It has been argued that this seemingly irrational sensitivity has served to discourage irresponsible speculation on the part of workers interested in studying religious behavior. But it has also tended to delimit the subject matter tackled by the psychologist of religion, and most obviously it has devastatingly curtailed the methodological perspective and interdisciplinary mood of the religious psychologist. It is here where contemporary humanistic psychology holds forth hope for a deeper and more significant religious psychology of the future, one more in keeping with the earliest projections of men like James and Starbuck.

HUMANISTIC PSYCHOLOGY AND THE PSYCHOLOGY OF RELIGION

The contemporary humanistic movement in psychology stresses an orientation which provides greater conceptual and methodological freedom than has been generally true in the history of American psychology. One of the leaders of the movement has suggested that the humanistic psychologist tends to be characterized by the following traits or tendencies:

Disavows as inadequate and even misleading descriptions of human functioning and experience based wholly or in large part on subhuman species.
Insists that meaning is more important than method in choosing problems for study, in designing and executing the studies, and in interpreting their results.
Gives primary concern to man's subjective experience and secondary concern to

his actions, insisting that this primacy of the subjective is fundamental in any human endeavor. . . .

Sees a constant interaction between "science" and "application" such that each constantly contributes to the other and the attempt rigidly to separate them is recognized as handicapping to both.

Is concerned with the individual, the exceptional, and the unpredicted rather than seeking only to study the regular, the universal, and the conforming. . . .

Seeks that which may expand or enrich man's experience and rejects the paralyzing perspective of nothing-but thinking. (Bugental, 1967)

Similar, but with even a broader scope, are the four characteristics espoused by the American Association for Humanistic Psychology, the professional organization which attempts to give identity to the new movement:

A centering of attention on the experiencing *person,* and thus on experience as the primary phenomenon in the study of man. Both theoretical explanations and overt behavior are considered secondary to experience itself and to its meaning to the person.

An emphasis on such distinctively human qualities as choice, creativity, valuation, and self-realization, as opposed to thinking about human beings in mechanistic and reductionistic terms.

An allegiance to meaningfulness in the selection of problems for study and of research procedures, and an opposition to a primary emphasis on objectivity at the expense of significance.

An ultimate concern with and valuing of the dignity and worth of man and an interest in the development of the potential inherent in every person. Central to this view is the person as he discovers his own being and relates to other persons and to social groups. (Buhler & Bugental, 1965)

Such intentions and sets—even recognizing the splinter-like nature of the movement—hold many potentially fruitful implications for the psychology of religion and for research in religion generally. For one thing, as has been noted, the psychology of religion has always been influenced directly by the *Zeitgeist* of the greater psychological community. As humanistic orientations become more and more a part of the climate of psychology proper, they, too, will influence the selection of research problems and the theoretical propensities of psychologists. Already, for example, one of the members of the humanistic group has recognized and critically prescribed the need for a new thrust in the psychological study of religion:

A humanistic psychology of religion would not lose Tillich's depth dimension; it would not lose the heart of that which is religious in the name of ease of observation and measurement. In short, contrary to the present dominant positivistic *Zeitgeist,* the humanistic psychological study of religion would deal in whatever way it could with the subjective meaning of life—with that which is existentially valid. . . . The traditional scientific approach to the psychological study of religion, one of the most important and ubiquitous characteristics of mankind, has not yet penetrated very deeply. It seems to me that the humanistic approach is more likely to probe the "inner man" because of its greater willingness to deal with the fullness of subjective experience via an all-encompassing phenomenology as opposed to a narrow, albeit more rigorous, empiricism. (Royce, 1967)

A second possible contribution to the enrichment of the psychology of religion, and one particularly relevant to scholars outside the psychological field itself, may be found in the promise of greater interdisciplinary involvement under the distended canopy of the humanistic orientation. In the past, the religious psychologist has tended to work exclusively within his own framework, drawing very little from the other sciences of religion and practically nothing from the humanistic disciplines. With the founding of the *Journal for the Scientific Study of Religion,* a bit more interdisciplinary sharing began; but the interdisciplinary activity of this movement has so far centered pretty much around the research of psychologists, sociologists, and anthropologists. The humanistic workers, the biblical scholars, religious educators, and the theologians have not generally been represented in any significant way.

One of the major reasons for the severe paucity of interdisciplinary research in the psychology of religion has been the tight conceptual framework of the psychologist of religion. Often controlled by a behavioristic bias, frequently motivated by a reductionistic wish, and sometimes intoxicated by a crass positivism, he has found it impossible to communicate with those disciplines which move outside the constellation of such assumptions—especially theology proper. Theology, including practical theology, has often recognized the potential contributions the behavioral sciences, including religious psychology, could make to its endeavors. But the conversations have been difficult and infrequent. The two communities have their own vocabularies and their own sets of assumptions. Even the psychology of religion itself, although frequently housed in the theological schools, has found it difficult to contribute significantly to the theological dialogue because its conceptual schema and its research activities have seemed irrelevant or superficial or to be too far removed from the deeper meanings of the religious quest.

A few current tendencies, however, demonstrate that the interdisciplinary approach is possible and productive. The explorations at recent American Psychological Association meetings where psychologists and theologians have entered into dialogue (Havens, 1968); the Gallahue Conference on Religion and Psychiatry where psychologists, philosophers, and theologians have considered the nature of the will (Lapsley, 1967); the recognition of the contents of the *Archiv für Religionspsychologie* by a German theological journal (Arnold, 1968); and the very recent attempt of the Secretariat of the National Conference of Catholic Bishops to elicit information from non-theological disciplines, including psychology, in the study of Catholic liturgy—are all signs that open conversations can fruitfully take place and may well be on the way.

A third result of the humanistic thrust may be the complete restructuring of the discipline itself. Traditionally, religious psychology has tended to walk a tightrope, carefully avoiding references to ontological questions and cautiously assuring everyone that it was descriptive only. Equally conservative was its preoccupation with religious experience, evading both the more "mundane" aspects of religion and also the more complex ones such as theological beliefs and systems.

Paul W. Pruyser makes this last point well when he writes that "the psychology of religion cannot confine itself to the private side of religious experience such as solitary prayer or mystical episodes, but must also come to grips with such public phenomena as theological treatises and liturgical processes" (Pruyser, 1968, p. 333). He would have the psychology of religion attend to these objects using essentially *psychological* categories. With a similar motive at work, but within the framework of the history of religion, Erwin R. Goodenough makes an opposite sort of observation:

To appraise the great body of religious data will demand that one rethink much of psychology, as one would have to do if faced with any other large body of unconsidered data. The business of the "psychology of religion" is not to fit religious experiences into the pigeonholes of Freud or Jung or into the categories of *Gestalt* or stimulus-response or any other, but rather to see what the data of religious experiences themselves suggest. (Goodenough, 1965, p. xi)

At first glance, these two prescriptions may appear at odds, but both are making a plea for a reconsideration of perspective for the psychology of religion. And I would suggest that their claims be extended even further by insisting that religious psychology might also relate recent cosmological arguments to its concerns. For example, the brilliant statements of Pierre Teilhard de Chardin (1959, 1964) and Sir Alistir Hardy (1965) in regard to evolutionary patterns of understanding, the stimulating insights of M. Polanyi (1958, 1964) on the nature of the scientific enterprise, the whole range of research being done in the discipline of world religions (Smith, 1963; Goodenough, 1965), the recent tantalizing suggestions of Edward D. Vogt (1968) for what he calls "religionics," and the suggestion of Bernard Spilka (1969) that we consider the formation of a "theological psychology," will need to be included in future work in the psychology of religion. If we are inclined to see the scope of the psychology of religion to include the study of those modes and projects of existence which meaningfully link this world with what is perceived to be unmanifest yet supremely worthful,[1] then we must indeed broaden our view of the purpose of religious psychology.

Undoubtedly, William James would be elated over the new possibilities for the future development of religious psychology, thanks partly at least to the humanistic stress beginning to be felt in psychology proper—a mood so characteristic of James himself. Just how influential this new liberalization in conceptualization and methodology will be in religious research remains to be seen. But certainly humanistic psychology has set ajar just a bit more the interdisciplinary doors, and it now appears that a new chapter in the history of the psychology of religion is beginning to be written.

[1] This concept of religious psychology will be developed fully in my forthcoming book *The Religious Value: A Religio-Psychological Understanding.*

Toward an Empirical Psychology of Religion

Bernard Spilka

Historically, man per se was the province of religion. The growth of biological science and medicine seemed to reduce human life to the level of a complex machine, while the advent of psychology tended to abstract man from his worldly and possible other-worldly contexts and turned him in upon himself. Thus it was that Freud (1928) theorized that religion was a normal product of psychic development to be cast aside with the coming of maturity. William James put faith in the pragmatic mold by stating: "If the hypothesis of God works satisfactorily . . . it is true" (James, 1908, pp. 299-300). As one wag put it, psychology first lost "its soul, then its mind, and then consciousness; but strangely enough it still behaves" (Baker, 1963, p. 1).

From "Images of Man and Dimensions of Personal Religion: Values for an Empirical Psychology of Religion," *Review of Religious Research*, 11 (1970), 171-82. Used by permission.

The foregoing remarks suggest an historical process by means of which man became dehumanized, as science usurped him from religion. In the framework of current psychology, this decline has resulted in the study of logical constructs and/or intervening variables, not of man himself. Hence, some troubled psychologists have asked in puzzlement, "Where is the perceiver in perception, and the learner in learning?" The shift from absolutist to relativistic physics further reduced the significance of man from at least a fairly well circumscribed object of study to one floating in a contingent universe.

The process of trivializing man has not occurred without resistance. Hume countered the Newtonian world view by asserting that "the science of man is the only solid foundation for the other sciences" (Becker, 1968, p. 22). In a similar vein, Diderot claimed that "it is the presence of man that renders natural existence interesting. . . . Man is the unique end from which we must begin and to which everything must return" (Becker, 1968, p. 3). Indeed this is the problem—to formulate a systematic view which without qualification acknowledges the human component in the social and behavioral sciences.

VALUATIONS IN THE PSYCHOLOGY OF RELIGION

Admiration of the empirical method by psychologists of religion has been mixed. The view that religious phenomena go far beyond what may be scientifically revealed is natural to most workers in this field, since their roots are originally within the religious domain itself. Data thus tend to take a back seat to extensive discussions which invariably do two things: (1) these efforts usually remain quite detached from research findings; and (2) there is a reluctance to grapple with factors which underlie this obvious ambivalence toward the objectification of religion. Moberg (1967) has raised somewhat overlapping considerations relative to the sociology of religion suggesting limits to social scientific research which demand serious reflection.

In essence, we may be observing the operation of apparently conflicting assumptions underlying social science and theology about the nature of man. Only recently has attention been focused on this problem (Chein, 1962; Doniger, 1962; McLaughlin, 1965; Pattison, 1965; Platt, 1965; Thomas, 1962). Unfortunately most of these attempts have not been directed at producing the kind of rapprochement which would result in a viable theoretical foundation for a research or empirically oriented psychology of religion. It is therefore felt that psychology and theology must be openly coordinated and integrated, or the prevailing confusion in the psychology of religion is likely to continue.

To accomplish this goal, the development of a "Theological-Psychology of Religion" may be necessary. As will be evident, this overlaps considerably with the notion of a humanistic psychology of religion (Royce, 1967; Strunk, 1970), and Pruyser's (1968) call for a restructured "Dynamic Psychology of Religion" to deal with both individual psychology and public theology and religious activity. The above reference to a "theological psychology" may, however, cause many social scientists to shudder, for theology is stereotyped as transcendental in concern. Novak counters this view and succintly describes the position taken here when he asserts that

. . . the astute reader of theological discourse will soon discover that every sentence in such discourse, however obliquely, refers to human actions, or dispositions, or programs. . . . The "Kingdom of God" . . . has an other-worldly, apocalyptic concomitant; yet, in its own right, it is a concrete this-worldly ideal. Theology studies ultimate vision of communal relationships and personal identity, insofar as these affect actual human experience. (Novak, 1968, p. 52)

The task is therefore clear—to explicate images of man's nature from psychology and theology, to reveal a growing commonality of outlook, and finally to demonstrate the ramifications this has for a systematic empirical and scientific psychology of religion—a theological one in essence.

PSYCHOLOGICAL IMAGES OF GOD

Models of human nature in psychology are by no means simple, even though the mainstream of psychological thought stresses a reductionistic mechanism. The sources for activating this mechanism are primarily of environmental origin as befits the powerful position of behaviorism. It is therefore not surprising that psychology is denoted, in many quarters, "behavioral" science. Sperry describes the "general stance of modern behavioral science" as "objective, mechanistic, materialistic, behavioristic, fatalistic, reductionistic" (Sperry, 1965, p. 76), while Bertalanffy speaks of this approach as "the robot model of human behavior" (Bertalanffy, 1968, p. 189). Chein summarizes these views as resting "on the false assumption that . . . every determinant of behavior is either a body-fact or an environment-fact" (Chein, 1962, p. 8).

When acceptance of a biological-vegetative framework is paramount, behavioral explanations become couched in terms of mechanistic contiguity, tension reduction and homeostasis. Tension is aroused first by tissue needs and physiological drives. If this is reduced in the presence of social elements, interpersonal values and skills are mechanically conditioned. It is also assumed that the energized person will remain active until the sources of his tension are sated. The goals of behavior are not growth, but equilibrium, "certain favorable steady states" (Stagner, 1961, p. 19).

This is the stuff learning theories are made of, and as McClelland (1955) poignantly observes, learning is synonymous with adjustment. One learns to adjust to the conditions that exist, not to change them. The content of what is learned is irrelevant, for we are process oriented—learning, thinking, perceiving which takes place *within* a vegetatively conceived being, whether rat or man. The "adjustment" model of life further implies the rightness of the circumstances in which one exists. The task is to fit in, conform, adjust to the prevailing environmental order. Man is primarily a passive being to be molded by his environment, hopefuly a benign one, a la Skinner (1948). The position is succinctly treated by the founder of Behaviorism, John B. Watson, who affirmed that "Behaviorism . . . takes the whole field of human adjustments as its own" (Watson, 1924, p. 11), but

psychology has little to do with setting of social standards of action, and nothing to do with moral standards. It does lie within her province to tell whether the individual man can act in accordance with such standards, and *how we may control him* or lead him *to act in harmony with them*" (Watson, 1919; p. 2; *italics* added).

The adjustment model, in verifying the correctness of the order of things (physical, social, political, and moral), strengthens the hand of clinical professionals in whom society has invested some power over persons defined as deviant. Here, adjustment models combine with those of medical-biological origin to connote maladjustment as "mental illness." The notion of illness supportively implies that the disturbed person is the relatively passive victim of circumstances—of an internal disease process. As an unwilling and unfortunate pawn of nature, the "patient" is put in the hands of the expert (psychiatrist, physician, or psychologist) for "treatment." Subvocally, the problem is an internal one, possibly somatogenic in origin, permitting the affected individual to be abstracted from the world for appropriate handling until he returns to an adjusted state of "mental health." Implied again is the correctness of the objective conditions that exist and compliance is the virtue to be sought and honored. Conformity and mental health are thus synonymous.

Recent years have witnessed the development of counter themes which deny these radical determinisms of either self or environment. Thus one hears of "humanistic" psychology (Bugental, 1967; Severin, 1965), "existential" psychology (May, 1961), and "action" psychology (Pratt & Tooley, 1967). The referent of normal gives way to ideal, and man the adjuster and reactor is supplanted by man the actor. The search is for an understanding of man in context: not in *interaction* where he is conceptualized as distinct and separate from all else, but in *transaction* where he is always part of something larger (Chein, 1962; Ittelson & Cantril, 1954). Passivity now yields to activity and control to freedom. The goals of this are evident in Pratt and Tooley's admonition that *"both* scientific and social progress are suspended when man's first agency, action, is idle" (Pratt & Tooley, 1964, p. 156).

Adopting this view, Ittelson and Kilpatrick (1966) and Bruner and Postman (1948, 1949) have repeatedly demonstrated that one's purposes, needs and expectations influence what is perceived. Even in the radically behavioristic domain of learning, action views of how people learn have been peripherally present since the early days of research in this area (Hilgard & Bower, 1966). In recent years, Mowrer's (1960, 1960a) willingness to utilize such language as "hope" and "joy" in his formulations illustrates how learning functions are increasingly being seen in the large and more realistic perspective of the total person.

Motivation theorists have also challenged mechanistic tension-reduction models of human behavior. Goldstein (1939), Rogers (1963), and Maslow (1962) speak of a force for positive growth, a tendency to "self-actualize" oneself, to utilize one's capacities to their fullest. Goldstein sees the inevitable development of self-actualization in an "urge to perfection" (Goldstein, 1963, p. 147).

A somewhat related view of human motivation has been proposed by Robert White (1959, 1960) and adopted by Bruner (1966). Emphasizing the motive to be competent, this position counters traditional conceptions of "mental health" and "adjustment." Effectiveness is the goal of activity, and this may imply some degree of adapting to circumstances plus efforts to change existing conditions. Each situation will therefore include behavior that, in the transactional view, is based on the creation of maximal opportunity for future self-determination and potential development. In like manner, Coleman asks "whether man is in fact an active and responsible agent with 'free will' or a puppet whose behavior is determined by forces beyond his control" (Coleman, 1960, p. 32).

IMAGES OF MAN IN RELIGION AND THEOLOGY

The distinction made in the title for this section is necessitated by the rather frequent and large discrepancies one observes between (1) the practice of established religion and (2) the body of doctrine justifying the existence of a church and individual faith. The transformation of the latter to the former is a cyclical tale of inspiration and institutionalization in which spirit is repeatedly submerged by pressure from vested power and the dehumanization of dogma and practice. In turn, there is the fractionation of formal religious bodies by a resurgence of creative and humanizing forces demanding spiritual relevance (Glock, 1964; O'Dea, 1961). Theologically man is the subject of religion, but institutionally he has often become its object.

In the course of religious formalization, churches tend more to mirror social forces than to mold them. As Marty states, "religious groups in our current society ordinarily serve as the *reactors*. They may hitchhike on secular elements of change" (Marty, 1964, p. 180). Moberg, in discussing "the new American piety," observes that "secularism . . . as a central theme prevails; 'the American Way' is the main creed" (Moberg, 1962, p. 63). The same position is affirmed by Herberg (1960), among many others (Gilkey, 1967; Johnson, 1952; Winter, 1961). Formal religion and the church thus act as agencies for social conformity and the suppression of deviance, but this need not be oppressively enforced. Identification with the church has a positive appeal of its own so that the faithful acquiesce willingly in reducing their freedom by valuing conforming modes of thought and action. Shades of *Walden Two* when Frazier explains, "We can achieve a sort of control under which the controlled, though they are following a code much more scrupulously than was ever the case under the old system, nevertheless *feel free*. . . . In that case the question of freedom never arises" (Skinner, 1948, p. 218).

Institutional religion and psychology frequently share a common view of man, the machine model. The former may do so reluctantly, but all too often in practice it values the status quo and resists change. Just as Skinner maintains that "the hypothesis that man is not free is essential to the application of scientific method to the study of human behavior," so many devout churchmen validate the inference that freedom may counter the "application of the religious method to man" (Skinner, 1953, pp. 447-48). Southard (1965) poignantly discusses the realization of these ideas in the methodology of "programming" as it may be applied in religious education. He points out that the philosophical assumptions and implications of such procedures are usually forgotten in the enthusiasm generated by the development of these rather exciting instructional methods.

At this juncture, it should be apparent that generalizations are being offered; by their very nature, such are inherently false. The foregoing positions are by no means exhaustively valid, any more so than those that follow. Nevertheless, they do describe in broadly accurate terms a reality that has been repeatedly confirmed.

Just as institutional religion implies an adjustment perspective, the theologies of the great religions have, at their core, maintained images of man that stress growth, freedom, capability, and action. The doctrine of free will embodies the idea of action in its fullest sense. Free will in Judaism "sees man creating a destiny that impinges on the infinite" (Baeck, 1948, p. 123). St. Thomas stresses the essential association between reason and freedom: "in that man is rational, it is necessary that he have free choice" (Aquinas, 1952, Vol. 1, p. 436). Niebuhr maintains "the essence of man in his freedom" (Niebuhr, 1942, p. 17).

Both psychologists and modern theologians are quite loath to accept the notion of a total unfettered freedom of human action that the doctrine of free will might imply. This view is well expressed by scholars whose feet are firmly planted within both psychology and theology. Thus, Van Kaam declares that "the human will is neither the absolute ruler imagined by the will-power Christian nor the product of libidinal and cultural determinism expounded by psychoanalysis and behaviorism" (Van Kaam, 1962, p. 5). Elsewhere he observes, "It is true that my behavior is conditioned, but I can influence the kind of conditioning by the meaning I freely impose on my tendencies and my environment" (Van Kaam, 1968, p. 125). Nuttin similarly avers that "a free act . . . is not the resultant pure and simple of a process governed by influences of environment and physiological factors, but there is also another principle behind it—the self-determination of a person" (Nuttin, 1962, p. 159).

In opposition to the conformist orientation of institutional religion, the tenet of free will is consonant with the position of action and humanistic psychology. Both strongly support the possibility of man shaping his situation and circumstances to elevate that which is *good* over that which is socially *right*.

THE TRANSACTIONAL PERSPECTIVE

We have seen an increasing awareness by psychologists of the role of an active organism rather than a reactive one throughout the realm of behavioral science. This viewpoint has long been established in traditional theology. A true appreciation of action must include the nature of the reality in which behavior is embedded; to accomplish this the term *transaction* has been introduced. Ittelson and Cantril define it as carrying

. . . the double implication (1) that all parts of the situation enter it [the total life situation] as active participants, and (2) that they owe their very existence as encountered in the situation to this fact of active participation and do not appear as already existing entities merely interacting with each other without affecting their own identity (Ittelson & Cantril, 1954, p. 3).

Pratt and Tooley emphasize the action aspect of the transactional-field when they claim that "man . . . can never be considered as more *nor* less than the creature *and* creator of his transactional world" (Pratt & Tooley, 1964, p. 52). Heschel (1965) and Van Kaam (1968) are fine expositors of a similar outlook in theology. Of the greatest significance is that these principles offer an heuristic framework for a "theological-psychology of religion."

DIRECTIONS FOR A "THEOLOGICAL-PSYCHOLOGY OF RELIGION"

Contemporary discussions of personality and mental disorder seem to stress three major aspects of the person-world transaction: (1) the relation of the individual to himself as illustrated by Organismic and Self-Concept theories and research (Combs & Snygg, 1959; Goldstein, 1959; Kelly, 1955; Wylie, 1961); (2) the relation of the person to the social world as found in Mirror-image, Social-Interpersonal, Biosocial, and Social Learning views (Goffman, 1959; Kluckhohn, Murray & Schneider, 1953; Rotter, 1954; Sullivan, 1953); and (3) the relation of the individual to an integrative ideal such as the search for meaning, realization, or some ultimate (Bertocci & Millard, 1963; Frankl, 1963, 1967; Ungersma, 1961). These approaches overlap, and most students of personality employ more than one in their formulations. Ideally, the effective personality demonstrates a realistically based high degree of self-regard, a positive pattern of social relationships involving appreciation of and respect for the individuality of others, and clear sense of identity which is associated with a progressive and constructive philosophy of life. The characteristics of Maslow's (1954) self-actualizing person may be conceptualized in this manner with surprisingly little effort.

The foregoing general dimensions of an adequate or better actualized personality have their counterparts within Judaeo-Christian theologies. Some explication of these referents from both the psychological and theological domains will now be undertaken to demonstrate their complementarity.

SELF-SIGNIFICANCE

In discussing "the purpose of creation," Maimonides (1956) identified self-knowledge with accurate comprehension of the nature of everything. His discussion of those "who constantly strive to choose that which is noble" is one facet of a positive evaluation of self through awareness of its likeness to that of the creator. Baeck also extols "the faith of man in himself," for through it, he asserts, "life acquires the strength to possess and choose itself; and that is its external-significance, its moral freedom" (Baeck, 1948, p. 189). Free will and effectiveness are thus premised on a positive and constructive self-understanding.

In Catholicism, St. Thomas (Aquinas, 1952: Part II of the Second Part; Questions 2, 25-27, 44) speaking of the virtues refers to an obligation to oneself in the sense of maintaining health, proper care of the body, and apparently mental well-being. Though this is the lowest of these positive obligations, it is still of basic importance in Thomistic philosophy.

Various Protestant theologians embrace similar elements. Beginning with Scripture, Brunner (1937) includes under the concept of love, love of self and neighbor. Niebuhr (1942) speaks of the "self in contemplation" and the "self in action." Like many psychologists whom he criticizes, Niebuhr carries out a rather detailed analysis of self-insight and adequacy.

Many of the analyses of self-love, self-regard, self-obligation and valuation found in religious literature bear a remarkable likeness to views held by members of the psychological-psychiatric community. Noteworthy here is the discussion offered by Kurt Goldstein on "Health as Value" (Goldstein, 1959, p. 179). This centers about "the essential significance of the phenomenon of health for man's self-realization." The centrality of self-oriented theories in contemporary psychology is well represented by the summary of twelve such positions in a currently popular text (Hall & Lindzey, 1957). The basic assumption underlying these views is that all behavior implies a concept of the self, and that to the extent this valuation is consistent, integrated, and positive, the individual responds in a mature and constructive manner. It is, of course, not fortuitous that scholars who espouse such views stress holistic-cognitive images of man and explicitly deny behavioristic conceptions. These treatments reveal the coincidence of theological and psychological outlooks, hence the ease with which they can be united in the construction of an empirical psychology of religion.

Operationally, the above identification recommends the assessment of individual religion with personality-type items and scales usually considered beyond the realm of religious measurement. Dittes (1969) strongly supports this approach; however, work relating faith to self and ego functions has been dubiously productive. It is fair to add that such efforts have not been well formulated. The asnwer may lie in simply using indices of self-adequacy as one set of religious criteria without regard to their association with other variables assessing spiritual orientation.

SOCIAL SIGNIFICANCE

From the golden rule and the social gospel to the death of God and situation ethics debates of today, man was and is primarily viewed as an ethical and social being. The scriptural admonition to "love thy neighbor as thyself" joins the high prescription for self-regard with a similar valuation of others. Rabbi Akiba termed this the highest ethical commandment (Cohen, 1968, p. 7). St. Thomas (1952) similarly places the obligation to others above that to the self. The moral core of faith is nowhere better clarified than in Einstein's assertion, "There is no higher religion than human service. To work for the common good is the greatest creed."

Social scientists increasingly regard man as first and foremost a social being. Mowrer claims that "the supreme anguish comes [for man] . . . from the rupturing of his sociality" (Mowrer, 1961, p. 126). He cites Karl Menninger to the effect that "mental illness must be a reaction to some kind of feeling of rupture with the social environment" (Mowrer, 1961, p. 126). Adler summarized his theory in view that "social interest and social cooperation are . . . the salvation of the individual" (Adler, 1929, p. 264). Two of the main criteria offered by Maslow and Mittelmann (1951)

131

for mental well-being are the "ability to satisfy the requirements of the group" and "adequate emancipation from the group or culture."

The likelihood of agreement between theologians and psychologists on the importance of one's social outlook and actions would not appear to be a source of difference, but rather of unity. Paul Johnson's position of Dynamic Interpersonalism (Johnson, 1966) demonstrates such congruence when he notes that "interpersonal psychology meets a theology of relationship." The psychological goal of social effectiveness and the religious aim of "following a moral life" therefore combine easily to provide additional footing for a "Theological-Psychology of Religion."

Research-wise, there is a massive literature examining the social perspectives of apparently religious individuals. Though the majority of churchgoers and those who assent to the dogma of faith appear to negate humanitarian motives (Kirkpatrick, 1949) and associate themselves with prejudices and discrimination (Allport, 1954, 1966; Dittes, 1970; Spilka & Reynolds, 1965), there is reason to believe that their religious outlook is a concensual one (Allen & Spilka, 1967). Great difficulty has been encountered trying to distinguish this form of personal religion from a committed faith. Dittes (1969), however, may again be correct when he recommends consideration of measures of social outlook and behavior as criteria of personal religion. The work of Allport & Ross (1967) and Allen & Spilka (1967) supports these as relevant additions to current criteria in the psychology of religion.

ULTIMATE SIGNIFICANCE

It was noted earlier that a third referent also provides for a similar combining of psychology and theology. This relates to active man's searching for some direction to make his life relevant and meaningful. Theologians have always perceived the aim of human existence as a search for ultimate significance, which is usually phrased in terms of God or the divine. One need not mention the wide variety of definitions and outlooks on what these concepts have come to mean; the central point is that whatever the referent, it is perceived as a fundamental striving for integration, direction, security, personal effectiveness, and above all, relation in an absolute sense. Aquinas thus tells us that "the proper end of faith is the joining of the human mind with divine faith" (Aquinas, 1952, p. 401). Within the Thomistic system, one's obligation or positive commandment to love God takes precedence above all else. It is as if comprehension of the purpose of life will always subsume proper appreciation of charity and self-regard. Classical Judaism also stresses that duty to God is primary to self- and other-love (Cohen, 1949); but according to Baeck, the problem is "not so much of what God is in himself, but what he means to man" (Baeck, 1948, p. 35).

Among modern Protestant theologians, Cox (1965) distinguishes the meaning- versus the naming-process relative to the concept of God. The former he feels to be a function of history and the social order. In a parallel vein, Cogley returns us to the position of Frankl (1963): namely, "the search for relevance will have to be a major mark of religion, the theological enterprise par excellence" (Cogley, 1968, p. 142).

As psychology discovers higher dimensions of motivation, some behavioral scientists see the identity of their concerns with those of religionists. Szasz claims that "life for most people is a continuous struggle, not for biological survival, but for a 'place in the sun,' 'peace of mind' or some other human value" (Szasz, 1960, p. 118). Rollo May also suggests that "people suffer personality breakdowns because they do not have meaning in their lives" (May, 1940, p. 13), and Viktor Frankl (1963) takes this "search for meaning" as the root of all human motivation. Jung (1962) saw such a lack of meaning as basically a problem "of finding a religious outlook on life."

Among recent developments, Elkind (1970) has constructed a cognitive theoretical approach which argues that religion is a natural product of normal mental growth. Somewhat similar is Blake's (1962) view that there exists a basic "spiritual" need within the human personality equivalent in significance to biological, personal, and social motivational categories.

Turning to the operational sphere, there are a number of referents for "this search for meaning." It is still quite valid to look for such a direction in adherence to established religious institutions. Strommen (1963) found this with respect to Lutheran youth. To the extent they are knowledgeable with regard to their faith and demonstrate behavioral commitment, their social and personal outlooks tend to be positive and progressive. Spilka and his associates have obtained similar evidence (Allen & Spilka, 1967; Spilka & Reynolds, 1965). Dean and Reeves (1962) also show how identification with a religious system may counter personal alienation. Moberg (1967) cautions against the view that these operational approaches exhaust all there is to religion. If his position is valid, we should recognize that the discrepancy between the correlations we obtain and that ideal of 1.00 with regard to the significance of faith may in part be a function of a "spiritual" component that constitutes the essence of religiosity.

One cannot disregard the meaningfulness to individuals of ideologies other than those found in the Judaeo-Christian tradition. The likelihood that these are not as independent of the latter as many might like to believe does merit exploration. It is more important to realize that the search for meaning and relevance may take a wide variety of forms, and the quest itself is both psychologically and theologically significant.

A PERSPECTIVE FOR RESEARCH

It is obviously true, as Dittes (1969) notes, that psychologists of religion will have to broaden their perspectives greatly in order to understand what they should be studying. Utilizing traditional criteria as an entree into the "religious search for meaning," it has been possible to demonstrate the multi-dimensional nature of personal religion (Spilka, Read, Allen, & Dailey, 1968).

Delineation of various religious forms provides a framework for under-standing their correlates in a contemporary and historical sense. In this way the self-, other-, and meaning-aspects of each type of personal religion can be operationaly denoted. The outcome would be a picture of different kinds of religionists, and criteria of faith would necessarily include a wide variety of personality, attitude and value measures not usually associated with the Psychology of Religion. This necessarily requires extensive theory develop-ment, something psychologists of religion have only weakly undertaken.

It should be evident that there are strong trends within psychology to resurrect man *in toto* from a misplaced emphasis on him as a compound of variables and fractionated processes. Current humanistic-psychological ver-sions of man *qua* man are basically similar to the views of man held in western theology. A natural step would be explicitly to combine common elements from theology and psychology. Hiltner's desire to treat "psychology as a theological discipline internal to theology itself" (Hiltner, 1962, p. 251) then would be a step closer to realization. The barriers between religion and psychology would be removed in the construction of a "Theological-Psychology of Religion" pertinent to both disciplines. This should elicit the kind of information and perspective that must form the groundwork for a true understanding of man; objective, yes, but not detached.

Bibliography

Ackerman, H. C. 1922. "The Differentiating Principle of Religion." *Journal of Philosophy*, 19, no. 12.

Adler, A. 1929. *The Science of Living*. Garden City, N.Y.: Garden City Publishing Co.

Alexander, F. 1930. *Psychoanalysis of the Total Personality*. Baltimore: Nervous & Mental Diseases Publishing Co.

Alexander, F., & French, T. M. 1946. *Psychoanalytic Therapy*. New York: Ronald Press.

Allen, R. O., & Spilka, B. 1967. "Committed and Consensual Religion: A Specification." *Journal for the Scientific Study of Religion*, 6, 191-208.

Allers, R. 1930. *Psychology of Character*. New York: Sheed and Ward.

Allers, R. 1933. *New Psychologies*. New York: Sheed and Ward.

Allers, R. 1940. *Successful Error*. New York: Sheed and Ward.

Allier, R. 1925. *La Psychologie de la Conversion*. Paris: Payot.

Allport, G. W. 1937. *Personality: A Psychological Interpretation*. New York: Henry Holt and Co.

Allport, G. W. 1944. *The Roots of Religion*. New York: National Council of the Protestant Episcopal Church.

Allport, G. W. 1950. *The Individual and His Religion: A Psychological Interpretation*. New York: The Macmillan Co.

Allport, G. W. 1954. *The Nature of Prejudice*. Cambridge, Mass.: Addison-Wesley.

Allport, G. W. 1966. "The Religious Context of Prejudice." *Journal for the Scientific Study of Religion*, 5, 447-57.

Allport, G. W., & Ross, J. M. 1967. "Personal Religious Orientation and Prejudice." *Journal of Personality and Social Psychology*, 5, 432-43.

Ames, E. S. 1910. *The Psychology of Religious Experience*. Boston: Houghton Mifflin Co.

Ames, E. S. 1921. "Religion in Terms of Social Consciousness." *Journal of Religion*, 1, 264-70.

Aquinas, Thomas. 1952. *Summa Theologica*, Vol. 2. Chicago: Encyclopaedia Britannica (Great Books of the Western World).

Arnold, Wilhelm. 1968. "Die Religionspsychologie auf neuen Wegen." *Münchener Theologische Zeitschrift*, 19, 46-49.

Arréat, M. 1903. *Le Sentiment Religieux en France*. Paris.

Aubrey, E. E. 1940. *Man's Search for Himself*. New York: Abingdon-Cokesbury.

Baeck, L. 1948. *The Essence of Judaism*. Rev. ed. New York: Schocken.

Baillie, J. 1926. *The Roots of Religion in the Human Soul*. New York: Doran.

Baker, R. A. 1963. *Psychology in the Wry*. New York: Van Nostrand.

Barry, F. R. 1923. *Christianity and Psychology*. London: Student Christian Movement Press.

Barry, F. R. 1923a. *St. Paul and Social Psychology*. New York: Oxford University Press.

Becker, E. 1968. *The Structure of Evil*. New York: George Braziller.

Behn, S. 1923. "Von methodischer Selbstbeobachtung in der Religionspsychlogie." *Archiv für Religionspsychologie,* 3, 160-89.

Benedict, Ruth. 1934. *Patterns of Culture.* Boston: Houghton Mifflin Co.

Bennett, C. A. 1926. "Religion and the Idea of the Holy." *Journal of Philosophy,* 23, 460-69.

Berkowitz, Morris T., & Johnson, J. Edmund. 1967. *Social Scientific Studies of Religion: A Bibliography.* Pittsburgh: University of Pittsburgh Press.

Bertalanffy, L. von. 1968. *General System Theory.* New York: George Braziller.

Bertocci, P. A., & Millard, R. M. 1963. *Personality and the Good.* New York: David McKay.

Blake, J. A. 1962. "Faith as a Basic Personality Need." *Pastoral Psychology,* 13, 43-47.

Bohne, G. 1922. *Die religiöse Entwicklung der Jugend in der Reifezeit.* Leipzig.

Boisen, A. T. 1936. *The Exploration of the Inner World.* Chicago: Willett, Clark.

Bonnell, J. S. 1938. *Pastoral Psychology.* New York: Abingdon.

Bovet, P. 1925. *Le Sentiment Religieux et la Psychologie de l'Enfant.* Neuchâtel & Paris: Ed. Delachaux et Niestlé.

Brillat-Savarin, T. 1826. *Physiology of Taste.* London: Boni & Liveright.

Brooks, C. H. 1923. *Christianity and Auto-suggestion.* New York: Dodd, Mead and Co.

Brotherston, B. W. 1924. "Religion and Instinct." *Journal of Religion,* 4, 504-21.

Brown, W. 1929. *Science and Personality.* New Haven: Yale University Press.

Bruner, J. S., & Postman, L. 1948. "Symbolic Value as an Organizing Factor in Perception." *Journal of Social Psychology,* 27, 203-8.

Bruner, J. S., & Postman, L. 1949. "On the Perception of Incongruity: A Paradigm." *Journal of Personality,* 18, 206-23.

Bruner, J. S. 1966. *Toward a Theory of Instruction.* Cambridge, Mass.: Harvard University Press.

Brunner, E. 1937. *The Divine Imperative.* London: Lutterworth Press.

Bugental, James F. T. (ed.) 1967. *Challenges of Humanistic Psychology.* New York: McGraw-Hill.

Buhler, Charlotte, & Bugental, James F. T. 1965. *American Association for Humanistic Psychology* (Brochure). San Francisco: American Association for Humanistic Psychology.

Burnham, W. H. 1891. "A Study of Adolescence." *Pedagogical Seminary,* 1, 175-95.

Butler, P. 1921. "Church History and Psychology of Religion." *American Journal of Psychology,* 32, 543-51.

Calverton, V. F. 1935. *The Passing of the Gods.* London: Allen.

Charbounier, V. 1874. *Maladies des mystiques.* Paris.

Chave, E. J. 1937. *Personality Development in Children.* Chicago: University of Chicago Press.

Chave, E. J. 1939. *Measure Religion—52 Experimental Forms.* Chicago: University of Chicago Press.

Chein, I. 1962. "The Image of Man." *Journal of Social Issues,* 18, 1-35.

Cherbonnier, E. La B. 1955. *Hardness of Heart.* Garden City, N.Y.: Doubleday & Co.

Clark, E. T. 1929. *The Psychology of Religious Awakening.* New York: The Macmillan Co.

Clark, Walter H. 1958. *The Psychology of Religion: An Introduction to Religious Experience and Behavior.* New York: The Macmillan Co.

Clavier, H. 1926. *L'Idée de Dieu chez l'Enfant.* Paris: Fischbacher.

Coe, G. A. 1900. *The Spiritual Life.* New York: Methodist Book Concern.

Coe, G. A. 1902. *The Religion of a Mature Mind.* New York: Fleming Revell Co.

Coe, G. A. 1916. *The Psychology of Religion.* Chicago: University of Chicago Press.

Cogley, J. 1968. *Religion in a Secular Age.* New York: Praeger.

Cohen, A. 1949. *Everyman's Talmud.* New York: Dutton.

Cohen, H. 1968. *Justice, Justice.* New York: Union of American Hebrew Congregations.

Coleman, J. C. 1960. *Personality Dynamics and Effective Behavior.* Chicago: Scott, Foresman.

Combs, A. W., & Snygg, D. 1959. *Individual Behavior.* Rev. ed. New York: Harper & Bros.

Conklin, E. S. 1929. *The Psychology of Religious Adjustment.* New York: The Macmillan Co.

Cooke, A. W. 1924. *Sacraments and Society: A Study of the Origin and Value of Rites in Religion.* Boston: Gorham.

Cox, H. 1965. *The Secular City.* New York: The Macmillan Co.

Cronbach, A. 1926. "Religion and Psychoanalysis." *Psychological Bulletin,* 23, 701-13.

Cutten, G. B. 1908. *The Psychological Phenomena of Christianity.* New York: Charles Scribner's Sons.

Daniels, A. H. 1895. "The New Life: A Study in Regeneration." *American Journal of Psychology,* 6, 61-103.

Dean, D. G., & Reeves, J. A. 1962. "Anomie: A Comparison of a Catholic and a Protestant Sample." *Sociometry,* 25, 209-12.

Dehn, G. 1923. *Die religiöse Gedankenwelt der Proletarierjugend in Selbstzeugnissen dargestellt.* Berlin: Furche-Verlag.

Delacroix, H. 1908. *Études d'Histoire et de Psychologie du Mysticisme.* Paris: Alcan.

Delacroix, H. 1922. *La Religion et la Foi.* Paris: Alcan.

Dewar, L., & Hudson, C. E. 1934. *Psychology for Religious Workers.* New York: Harper & Bros.

Dicks, R. L., & Cabot, R. C. 1936. *The Art of Ministering to the Sick.* New York: The Macmillan Co.

Dicks, R. L. 1945. *Pastoral Work and Personal Counseling.* New York: The Macmillan Co.

Dittes, J. E. 1969. "Secular Religion: Dilemma of Churches and Researcher." *Review of Religious Research,* 10, 65-81.

Dittes, J. E. 1970. "The Psychology of Religion." In E. Aronson and G. Lindzey (eds.), *Handbook of Social Psychology,* Vol. 5, Cambridge, Mass.: Addison-Wesley, 602-59.

Doniger, S. 1962. *The Nature of Man in Theological and Psychological Perspective.* New York: Harper & Row.

Durkheim, Emile. 1915. *The Elementary Forms of the Religious Life: A Study in Religious Sociology.* New York: The Macmillan Co.

Elkind, D. 1970. "The Origins of Religion in the Child." *Review of Religious Research,* 12, 35-42.

Elliott, H. S., & Elliott, G. L. 1936. *Solving Personal Problems.* New York: Henry Holt & Co.

Elliott, H. S., & Elliott, G. L. 1941. *Can Religious Education be Christian?* New York: The Macmillan Co.

Elliott, H. S. 1927. *The Bearing of Psychology upon Religion.* New York: Association Press.

Feuerbach, L. 1957. *The Essence of Christianity.* New York: Harper & Bros.

Flower, J. C. 1927. *An Approach to the Psychology of Religion.* New York: Harcourt, Brace and Co.

Forsyth, D. 1935. *Psychology and Religion.* London: Watts.

Frankl, V. E. 1963. *Man's Search for Meaning.* New York: Washington Square Press.

Frankl, V. E. 1967. *The Doctor and the Soul.* New York: Bantam Books.

Frazer, J. G. 1915. *The Golden Bough: A Study in Magic and Religion.* New York: The Macmillan Co.

Frazer, J. G. 1927. *The Gorgon's Head.* London: Macmillan and Co.

Frazer, J. G. 1935. *The Golden Bough.* 3rd ed. London: Macmillan and Co.

Freud, S. 1918. *From the History of an Infantile Neurosis.* In Vol. III, *Collected Papers.* London: Hogarth Press, 1933.

Freud, S. 1928. *The Future of an Illusion,* trans. W. D. Robson-Scott, Horace Liveright, and the Institute of Psychoanalysis. (International Psychoanalytic Library, no. 15.) London: Hogarth Press.

Freud, S. 1930. *Civilization and Its Discontents.* New York: W. W. Norton and Co.

Freud, S. 1953. *Interpretation of Dreams.* Vols. IV and V in *The Standard Edition of the Complete Psychological Works of Sigmund Freud,* trans. James Strachey *et al.* London: Hogarth Press.

Freud, S. 1955. *Totem and Taboo* (1913). In Vol. XIII of *The Standard Edition of the Complete Psychological Works of Sigmund Freud,* trans. James Strachey *et al.* London: Hogarth Press.

Fromm, E. 1947. *Man for Himself.* New York: Rinehart & Co.

Gilkey, L. 1967. "Social and Intellectual Sources of Contemporary Protestant Theology in America." *Daedalus,* 96, 69-98.

Girgensohn, K. 1921. *Der seelische Aufbau des religiösen Erlebens.* Leipzig: Hirzel.

Girgensohn, K. 1923. *Religionspsychologien, Religionswissenschaft und Religion*. Leipzig: Antrittsvorlesung.

Girgensohn, K. 1924. "Die Erscheinungsweisen religiöser Gedanken" *Ber. u.d. Kongress f. exper. Psychol.*

Glock, C. Y. 1964. "The Role of Deprivation in the Origin and Evolution of Religious Groups." In R. Lee and M. E. Marty (eds.), *Religion and Social Conflict*. New York: Oxford University Press, 24-36.

Godin, A. (ed.) 1964. *From Religious Experience to a Religious Attitude*. Brussels, Belgium: Lumen Vitae Press.

Goffman, E. 1959. *The Presentation of Self in Everyday Life*. Garden City, N. Y.: Doubleday & Co.

Goldstein, K. 1939. *Organism*. New York: American Book Co.

Goldstein, K. 1959. "Health as Value" In A. H. Maslow (ed.), *New Knowledge in Human Values*. New York: Harper & Row, 178-88.

Goldstein, K. 1963. *Human Nature in the Light of Psychopathology*. New York: Schocken.

Goodenough, E. R. 1965. *The Psychology of Religious Experience*. New York: Basic Books.

Grensted, L. W. 1930. *Psychology and God*. New York: Longmans, Green and Co.

Gulick, L. 1897-98. "Sex and Religion." *Association Outlook*.

Hadfield, J. A. 1925. *Psychology and Morals*. New York: McBride.

Hall, C. S., & Lindzey, G. 1957. *Theories of Personality*. New York: Wiley.

Hall, G. S. 1904. *Adolescence*. 2 vols. New York: D. Appleton.

Hardman, O. (ed.) 1925. *Psychology and the Church*. New York.: The Macmillan Co.

Hardy, Alistir C. 1965. *The Living Stream*. New York: Collins.

Harman, N. B. 1935. *Science and Religion*. New York: The Macmillan Co.

Hartshorne, H. 1933. *Character in Human Relations*. New York: Charles Scribner's Sons.

Havens, J. (ed.) 1968. *Psychology and Religion: A Contemporary Dialogue*. New York: Van Nostrand.

Hecker, J. F. 1936. *Religion and a Changing Civilization*. London: Lane.

Heiler, F. 1923. *Das Gebet: Eine religionsgeschichtliche und religionspsychologische Untersuchung*. München: Verlag von Ernst Reinhardt.

Heiler, F. 1932. *Prayer*. New York: Oxford University Press.

Herberg, W. 1955. *Protestant, Catholic, Jew*. Garden City, N. Y.: Doubleday & Co.

Herberg, W. 1960. *Protestant, Catholic, Jew*. Rev. ed. Garden City, N.Y.: Doubleday & Co.

Heschel, A. J. 1965. *Who Is Man?* Stanford, Calif.: Stanford University Press.

Hickman, F. S. 1926. *Introduction to the Psychology of Religion*. New York: Abingdon.

Hilgard, E. R., & Bower, G. H. 1966. *Theories of Learning*. 3rd ed. New York: Appleton-Century-Crofts.

Hiltner, S. (ed.) 1939. *Christianity and Mental Hygiene*. New York: Federal Council of Churches.

Hiltner, S. 1947. "The Psychological Understanding of Religion." *Crozer Quarterly*, 24, 3-26.

Hiltner, S. 1958. *Preface to Pastoral Theology*. Nashville: Abingdon Press.

Hiltner, S. 1962. "Conclusion: The Dialogue on Man's Nature." In S. Doniger (ed.), *The Nature of Man*. New York: Harper & Row.

Hirsch, M. 1922. "Die seelische Struktur des religiösen Erlebnisses." *Giessener Dissertation*.

Hocking, W. E. 1912. *The Meaning of God in Human Experience*. New Haven: Yale University Press.

Hocking, W. E. 1918. *Human Nature and Its Remaking*. New Haven: Yale University Press.

Hocking, W. E. 1921. "Is the Group Spirit Equivalent to God for All Practical Purposes?" *Journal of Religion*, 1, 482-96.

Hocking, W. E. 1923. *Human Nature and Its Remaking*. Rev. ed. New Haven: Yale University Press.

Hocking, W. E. 1923a. "Illicit Naturalizing of Religion." *Journal of Religion*, 3, 561-89.

Hoeffding, H. 1906. *Philosophy of Religion*. New York: The Macmillan Co.

Hoeffding, H. 1923. *Erlebnis und Deutung. Eine vergleichende Studie zur Religionspsychologie*. Stuttgart: Frommann.

Hofmann, H. 1955. Review of C. G. Jung, *Answer to Job*. *The Christian Century*, LXXII, 452-53.

Hofmann, P. 1925. *Das Religiöse Erlebnis: Seine Struktur, seine Typen und sein Wahrheitsanspruch.* Charlottenburg: Pan-Verlag.

Hollington, J. D. 1938. *Psychology Serving Religion.* New York: Abingdon.

Holman, C. T. 1932. *The Cure of Souls.* Chicago: University of Chicago Press.

Holman, C. T. 1942. *Getting Down to Cases.* New York: The Macmillan Co.

Horney, Karen, 1937. *Neurotic Personality of Our Times.* New York: W. W. Norton and Co.

Horney, Karen. 1939. *New Ways in Psychoanalysis.* New York: W. W. Norton and Co.

Horney, Karen. 1945. *Our Inner Conflicts.* New York: W. W. Norton and Co.

Horton, W. M. 1931. *A Psychological Approach to Theology.* New York: Harper & Bros.

Hudson, C. E. 1923. *Recent Psychology and the Christian Religion.* New York: Doran.

Hughes, T. H. 1933. *The New Psychology and Religious Experience.* London: George Allen & Unwin.

Hughes, T. H. 1937. *Philosophic Basis of Mysticism.* New York: Charles Scribner's Sons.

Hughes, T. H. 1937a. *Psychology and Religious Origins.* New York: Charles Scribner's Sons.

Hughes, T. H. 1941. *Psychology of Preaching and Pastoral Work.* New York: The Macmillan Co.

Hughes, T. H. 1942. *Psychology and Religious Truth.* New York: The Macmillan Co.

Hylan, J. P. 1901. *Public Worship.* Chicago: Open Court.

Inge, W. R. 1909. *Faith and Its Psychology.* London: Duckworth.

Ittelson, W. H. & Cantril, H. 1954. *Perception: A Transactional Approach.* Garden City, N. Y.: Doubleday & Co.

Ittelson, W. H. & Kilpatrick, F. L. 1966. "Experiments in Perception." In S. Coopersmith (ed.), *Frontiers of Psychological Research.* San Francisco: W. H. Freeman.

James. W. 1902. *The Varieties of Religious Experience.* New York: Longmans, Green and Co.

James. W. 1908. *Pragmatism.* New York: Longmans, Green & Co.

Jastrow, M. 1935. *Wish and Wisdom: Episodes in the Vagaries of Belief.* New York: Appleton-Century-Crofts.

Johnson, F. E. 1952. "Do Churches Exert Significant Influence on Public Morality?" *The Annals of the American Academy of Political and Social Science,* 280, 125-32.

Johnson, P. E. 1945. *Psychology of Religion.* Nashville: Abingdon Press.

Johnson, P. E. 1957. *Personality and Religion.* Nashville: Abingdon Press.

Johnson, P. E. 1959. *Psychology of Religion.* Rev. ed. Nashville: Abingdon Press.

Johnson, P. E. 1966. "The Trend Toward Dynamic Interpersonalism." *Religion in Life,* 35, 751-59.

Jones, E. 1951. "Psychoanalysis and the Christian Religion." In *Essays in Applied Psychoanalysis,* Vol. II. (International Psychoanalytic Library, no. 41.) London: Hogarth Press.

Jones, E. 1951a. "A Psychoanalytic Study of the Holy Ghost." In *Essays in Applied Psychoanalysis,* Vol. II. (International Psychoanalytic Library, no. 41). London: Hogarth Press.

Jones, E. 1951b. "The Psychology of Religion." In *Essays in Applied Psychoanalysis,* Vol. II. (International Psychoanalytic Library, no. 41.) London: Hogarth Press.

Josey, C. C. 1927. *The Psychology of Religion.* New York: The Macmillan Co.

Jung, C. G. 1916. *Analytical Psychology.* New York: Moffatt, Yard.

Jung, C. G. 1923. *Psychological Types.* New York: Harcourt, Brace and Co.

Jung, C. G. 1928. *Two essays on Analytical Psychology.* New York: Harcourt, Brace and Co.

Jung, C. G. 1933. *Modern Man in Search of a Soul.* New York: Harcourt, Brace and Co.

Jung, C. G. 1938. *Psychology and Religion.* New Haven: Yale University Press.

Jung, C. G. 1939. *Integration of the Personality.* New York: Farrar & Rinehart.

Jung, C. G. 1952. Foreword to V. White, *God and the Unconscious.* London: Harvill Press.

Jung, C. G. 1954. *Answer to Job.* London: Routledge & Kegan Paul.

Kelly, G. A. 1955. *Psychology of Personal Constructs.* New York: W. W. Norton and Co.

King, I. 1905. "The Differentiation of the Religious Consciousness." *Psychological Review,* Monograph Supplement (January).

King, I. 1910. *The Development of Religion.* New York: The Macmillan Co.

Kirkpatrick, G. 1949. "Religion and Humanitarianism: A Study of Institutional Implication." *Psychological Monographs,* 63 (9).

Kluckhohn, C., Murray, H. A., & Schneider, D. M. 1953. *Personality in Nature, Society, and Culture.* 3rd ed. New York: Alfred A. Knopf.

Koepp, W. 1920. *Einführung in das Studium der Religionspsychologie.* Tübingen: Mohr.

Koffka, K. 1924. *Growth of the Mind.* New York: Harcourt, Brace and Co.

Koffka, K. 1935. *Principles of Gestalt Psychology.* New York: Harcourt, Brace and Co.

Köhler, W. 1929. *Gestalt Psychology.* New York: Liveright.

Köhler, W. 1942. *Dynamics in Psychology.* New York: Faber.

Kunkel, F. 1936. *Conquer Yourself.* New York: Ives Washburn.

Kunkel, F. 1938. *Character, Growth, Education.* Philadelphia: J. B. Lippincott Co.

Kunkel, F., & Dickerson, R. E. 1940. *How Character Develops.* New York: Charles Scribner's Sons.

Kunkel, F. 1943. *In Search of Maturity.* New York: Charles Scribner's Sons.

Lancaster, E. G. 1895. "The Psychology and Pedagogy of Adolescence." *Pedagogical Seminary,* 5, 61-128.

Langley, G. H. 1924. "Interpretation of Religious Experience." *Hibbert Journal,* 22, 644-63.

Lapsley, James N. (ed.) 1967. *The Concept of Willing.* Nashville: Abingdon Press.

Lawton, G. 1932. *The Drama of Life After Death.* New York: Henry Holt & Co.

LeBon, G. 1913. *Psychology of Revolution.* New York: Putnam.

Lejeune, P. 1899. *Introduction à la vie mystique.* Paris: Benyiger.

Leuba, J. H. 1896. "The Psychology of Religious Phenomena." *American Journal of Psychology,* 7, 309-85.

Leuba, J. H. 1901. "Introduction to a Psychological Study of Religion." *Monist,* 11, 195-255.

Leuba, J. H. 1901a. "The Contents of Religious Consciousness." *Monist,* 11, 535-73.

Leuba, J. H. 1901b. "Religion: Its Impulses and Its Ends." *Bibliotheca Sacra,* 58, 758-69.

Leuba, J. H. 1902. "Tendances Fondamentales des Mystiques Chrétiens." *Revue Philosophique,* 54, 1-36; 441-87.

Leuba, J. H. 1903. "The State of Death." *American Journal of Psychology,* 14, 397-409.

Leuba, J. H. 1904. "Faith." *American Journal of Religious and Psychological Education,* 1, 65-112.

Leuba, J. H. 1904a. "The Field and Problems of the Psychology of Religion." *American Journal of Religious and Psychological Education,* 1, 155-67.

Leuba, J. H. 1905. "On the Psychology of a Group of Christian Mystics." *Unid,* 14, 15-27.

Leuba, J. H. 1906. "Fear, Awe, and the Sublime in Religion." *American Journal of Religious and Psychological Education,* 2, 1-23.

Leuba, J. H. 1907. "Religion as a Factor in the Struggle for Life." *American Journal of Religious and Psychological Education,* 2, 307-43.

Leuba, J. H. 1912. *A Psychological Study of Religion.* New York: The Macmillan Co.

Leuba, J. H. 1916. *The Belief in God and Immortality.* Chicago: Open Court.

Leuba, J. H. 1921. *The Belief in God and Immortality.* 2nd ed. Chicago: Open Court.

Leuba, J. H. 1925. *The Psychology of Religious Mysticism.* New York: Harcourt, Brace and Co.

Leuba, J. H. 1926. "The Psychology of Religion as Seen by Representatives of the Christian Religion." *Psychological Bulletin,* 23, 714-22.

Lewin, K. 1935. *Dynamic Theory of Personality.* New York: McGraw-Hill.

Lewin, K. 1936. *Principles of Topological Psychology.* New York: McGraw-Hill.

Lewin, K. 1938. *Conceptual Representation and the Measurement of Psychological Forces.* Durham, N. C.: Duke University Press.

Lidgett, J. S. 1923. "Religion and Psychology." *Cont. Rev.,* 124, 601-10.

Liebman, J. L. 1946. *Peace of Mind.* New York: Simon & Schuster.

Ligon, E. M. 1935. *The Psychology of Christian Personality.* New York: The Macmillan Co.

Ligon, E. M. 1940. *Their Future Is Now.* New York: The Macmillan Co.

Lutoslawski, W. 1923. "The Conversion of a Psychologist." *Hibbert Journal,* 21, 697-710.

McClelland, D. C. 1955. "The Psychology of Mental Content Reconsidered." *Psychological Review,* 62, 297-302.

McKenzie, J. G. 1929. *Souls in the Making.* New York: The Macmillan Co.

McKenzie, J. G. 1940. *Psychology, Psychotherapy and Evangelicalism.* New York: The Macmillan Co.

McLaughlin, B. 1965. "Values in Behavioral Science." *Journal of Religion and Health,* 4, 258-79.

Maimonides, M. 1956. *The Guide for the Perplexed.* New York: Dover.

Marcel, G. 1944. *Homo Viator: prolégomènes a une métaphysique de l'espérance.* Paris: Aubier, Editions Montaigne.

Martin, E. D. 1924. *The Mystery of Religion.* New York: Harper & Bros.

Marty, M. E. 1964. "Epilogue: The Nature and Consequences of Social Conflict for Religious Groups." In R. Lee and M. E. Marty (eds.), *Religion and Social Conflict.* New York: Oxford University Press.

Maslow, A. H., & Mittelmann, B. 1951. *Principles of Abnormal Psychology.* Rev. ed. New York: Harper & Bros.

Maslow, A. H. 1954. *Motivation and Personality.* New York: Harper & Bros.

Maslow, A. H. 1962. *Toward a Psychology of Being.* New York: Van Nostrand.

Masserman, J. H. 1955. *The Practice of Dynamic Psychiatry.* Philadelphia: W. B. Saunders Co.

Mathews, S. 1923. "Theology from the Point of View of Social Psychology." *Journal of Religion,* 3, 337-51.

May, R. 1939. *Art of Counseling.* Nashville: Abingdon Press.

May, R. 1940. *Springs of Creative Living.* Nashville: Abingdon Press.

May, R. (ed.) 1961. *Existential Psychology.* New York: Random House.

Meehl, P. 1957. "Religion and the Maintenance of Mental Health." In *Society's Stake in Mental Health,* pp. 52-61. Minneapolis: Social Science Research Center, University of Minnesota.

Meissner, W. W. 1961. *Annotated Bibliography in Religion and Psychology.* New York: Academy of Religion and Mental Health.

Menninger, K. A. 1937. *The Human Mind.* New York: Alfred A. Knopf.

Menninger, K. A. 1938. *Man Against Himself.* New York: Harcourt, Brace and Co.

Menninger, K. A. 1942. *Love Against Hate.* New York: Harcourt, Brace and Co.

Menniger, K. A. 1952. *A Manual for Psychiatric Case Study.* New York: Grune & Stratton.

Moberg, D. O. 1962. *The Church as a Social Institution.* Englewood Cliffs, N. J.: Prentice-Hall.

Moberg, D. O. 1967. "The Encounter of Scientific and Religious Values Pertinent to Man's Spiritual Nature." *Sociological Analysis,* 28, 22-33.

Moore, T. V. 1926. *Dynamic Psychology.* Philadelphia: J. B. Lippincott Co.

Moore, T. V. 1943. *Nature and Treatment of Mental Disorders.* New York: Grune & Stratton.

Moore, T. V. 1944. *Personal Mental Hygiene.* New York: Grune & Stratton.

Moses, J. 1906. *Pathological Aspects of Religion.* London: Strechert.

Mower, O. H. 1960. *Learning Theory and Behavior.* New York: Wiley.

Mower, O. H. 1960a. *Learning Theory and the Symbolic Processes.* New York: Wiley.

Mower, O. H. 1961. *The Crisis in Psychiatry and Religion.* New York: Van Nostrand.

Mudge, E. L. 1923. *The God Experience.* Cincinnati: Caxton.

Mueller-Freienfels, R. 1920. *Psychologie der Religion.* 2 vols. (Sammlung Göschen, Bd. 805-806.) Berlin.

Murray, H. A. 1938. *Explorations in Personality.* New York: Oxford University Press.

Murray, H. A., & Tomkins, S. S. 1943. *Contemporary Psychology.* Cambridge, Mass.: Harvard University Press.

Murray, J. A. C. 1938. *An Introduction to a Christian Psychotherapy.* New York: Charles Scribner's Sons.

Murray, Margaret. 1921. *The Witch Cult in Western Europe.* New York: Oxford University Press.

Murray, Margaret 1933. *The God of the Witches.* London: Low.

Niebuhr, R. 1942. *The Nature and Destiny of Man: A Christian Perspective.* New York: Charles Scribner's Sons.

Northridge, W. L. 1924. *Recent Psychology and Evangelistic Preaching.* London: Epworth Press.

Novak, M. 1968. "Secular Saints." *The Center Magazine*, 1, 51-59.
Nuttin, J. 1962. *Psychoanalysis and Personality*. New York: New American Library.

O'Dea, T. F. 1961. "Five Dilemmas in the Institutionalization of Religion." *Journal for the Scientific Study of Religion*, 1, 30-39.
Otto, R. 1923. *The Idea of the Holy*. New York: Oxford University Press.
Otto, R. 1957. *Mysticism East and West*. New York: Meridian Books.

Pattison, E. M. 1965. "Contemporary Views of Man in Psychology." *Journal of Religion and Health*, 4, 353-66.
Petrullo, V. 1934. *The Diabolic Root*. Philadelphia: University of Pennsylvania Press.
Pfister, O. 1923. *Some Applications of Psychoanalysis*. London: George Allen & Unwin.
Pfister, O. 1928. *Psychoanalyse und Weltanschauung*. Leipzig: Internationaler Psychoanalytischer Verlag.
Pfister, O. 1944. *Christianity and Fear*. New York: The Macmillan Co.
Pfister, O. 1963. *Psychoanalysis and Faith*. New York: Basic Books.
Plant, J. S. 1938. *Emotions of the Child*. Iowa City: University of Iowa Press.
Platt, J. R. (ed.) 1965. *New Views of the Nature of Man*. Chicago: University of Chicago Press.
Polanyi, M. 1957. "Problem Solving." *British Journal of the Philosophy of Science*, 8, 89-103.
Polanyi, M. 1958. *Personal Knowledge*. Chicago: University of Chicago Press.
Polanyi, M. 1964. *Science, Faith and Society*. Chicago: University of Chicago Press.
Pratt, J. B. 1907. *The Psychology of Religious Belief*. New York: The Macmillan Co.
Pratt, J. B. 1920. *The Religious Consciousness*. New York: The Macmillan Co.
Pratt, S., & Tooley, J. 1964. "Contract Psychology and the Actualizing Transactional-field." *International Journal of Social Psychiatry*, 1, 51-69.
Pratt, S. & Tooley, J. 1967. "Action Psychology," *Journal of Psychological Studies*, 15, 137-231.
Price, E. J. 1924. "The Limitations of the Psychology of Religion." *Hibbert Journal*, 22, 664-73.
Pruyser, P. W. 1958. "Is Mental Health Possible?" *Bulletin of the Menninger Clinic*, 23, 58-66.
Pruyser, P. W. 1959. "The Idea of Destiny." *Hibbert Journal*, 57, 380-85.
Pruyser, P. W. 1968. *A Dynamic Psychology of Religion*. New York: Harper & Row.
Pym, T. W. 1922. *Psychology and the Christian Life*. New York: Doubleday.
Pym, T. W. 1925. *More Psychology and the Christian Life*. New York: Doran.
Pym, T. W. 1928. *Spiritual Direction*. New York: Morehouse.
Pym, T. W. 1930. *Parson's Dilemmas*. New York: Morehouse.

Raglan, F. R. S. 1936. *The Hero*. London: Methuen.
Rank, O. 1929. *Trauma of Birth*. New York: Harcourt, Brace and Co.
Rank, O. 1932. *Art and Artist*. New York: Alfred A. Knopf.
Rank, O. 1932a. *Modern Education*. New York: Alfred A. Knopf.
Rank, O. 1936. *Truth and Reality*. New York: Alfred A. Knopf.
Rank, O. 1936a. *Will Therapy*. New York: Alfred A. Knopf.
Reik, T. 1936. *Surprise and the Psychoanalyst*. London: Routledge.
Rhine, J. B. 1935. *Extra-Sensory Perception*. Boston: Society for Psychic Research.
Rogers, C. R. 1939. *Clinical Treatment of the Problem Child*. Boston: Houghton Mifflin.
Rogers, C. R. 1942. *Counseling and Psychotherapy*. Boston: Houghton Mifflin.
Rogers, C. R., & Wallen, J. L. 1946. *Counseling with Returned Servicemen*. New York: McGraw-Hill.
Rogers, C. R. 1963. "The Actualizing Tendency in Relation to 'Motives' and to Consciousness." In M. R. Jones (ed.), *Nebraska Symposium on Motivation*. Lincoln: University of Nebraska Press.
Rose, A. N. 1924. "Psychology and Spiritual Miracles." *Cont. Rev.*, 125, 485-96.
Rotter, J. B. 1954. *Social Learning and Clinical Psychology*. Englewood Cliffs, N. J.: Prentice-Hall.
Royce, J. R. 1967. "Mentaphoric Knowledge and Humanistic Psychology." In *Challenges of Humanistic Psychology*. New York: McGraw-Hill.

Sanctis, S. de. 1927. *Religious Conversion*. New York: Harcourt, Brace and Co.

Schaub, E. L. 1922. "The Present Status of the Psychology of Religion." *Journal of Religion*, 2, 362-79.

Schaub, E. L. 1924. "The Psychology of Religion in America During the Past Quarter Century." *Journal of Religion*, 4, 113-34.

Schilp, A. (ed.) 1939. *The Philosophy of John Dewey*. Evanston, Ill.: Northwestern University Press.

Schleiermacher, F. E. D. 1928. *The Christian Faith*. Trans. and ed. H. R. MacKintosh and J. S. Stewart. Edinburgh: T. & T. Clark.

Selbie, W. B. 1924. *The Psychology of Religion*. Oxford: Clarendon Press.

Severin, F. T. 1965. *Humanistic Viewpoints in Psychology*. New York: McGraw-Hill.

Sheldon, H. C. 1921. "The Psychology of Religion Interrogated." *Princeton Theological Review*, 20, 41-56.

Sherrill, L. J. 1945. *Guilt and Redemption*. Richmond: John Knox Press.

Shoben, E. J., Jr. 1957. "Toward a Concept of the Normal Personality." *American Psychologist*, XII, 183-89.

Simpson, H. J. 1945. *Pastoral Care of Nervous People*. New York: Morehouse-Gorham Co.

Skinner, B. F. 1948. *Walden Two*. New York: The Macmillan Co.

Skinner, B. F. 1953. *Science and Human Behavior*. New York: The Macmillan Co.

Smith, Wilfred C. 1963. *The Meaning and End of Religion*. New York: The Macmillan Co.

Southard, E. E. 1922. *The Kingdom of Evils*. New York: The Macmillan Co.

Southard, S. 1965. "The Christian Individual in a 'Programmed' World." *Religious Education*, 60, 209-14; 243.

Sperry, R. W. 1965. "Mind, Brain, and Humanist Values." In J. R. Platt (ed.), *New Views of Human Nature*. Chicago: University of Chicago Press.

Spilka, B., & Reynolds, J. F. 1965. "Religion and Prejudice: A Factor-Analytic Study." *Review of Religious Research*, 6, 163-68.

Spilka, B.; Reed, Sonya J.; Allen, R. O.; & Dailey, Kathryn A. 1968. "Specificity vs. Generality: The Criterion Problem in Religious Measurement." Paper presented at the 1968 Convention of the American Association for the Advancement of Science, Dallas, Texas, Dec. 30.

Spilka, B. 1969. "Conceptions of Man and Dimensions of Personal Religion." Paper read at the Institute on the Psychology of Religion, Catholic University, Washington, D.C., June 17.

Spranger, E. 1925. *Psychologie des Jugendalters*. Leipzig: Quelle & Meyer.

Staehlin, W. 1921. "Die Wahrheitsfrage in der Religionspsychologie." *Archiv für Religionspsychologie*, 1, 136-59.

Stagner, R. 1937. *Psychology of Personality*. New York: McGraw-Hill.

Stagner, R. 1961. *Psychology of Personality*. 3rd ed. New York: McGraw-Hill.

Starbuck, E. D. 1903. *The Psychology of Religion*. New York: Charles Scribner's Sons.

Starbuck, E. D. 1921. "The Intimate Senses as Sources of Wisdom." *Journal of Religion*, 1, 129-45.

Stavenhagen, K. 1925. *Absolute Stellungnahmen: Eine ontologische Untersuchung ueber das Wesen der Religion*. Erlangen: Verlag der Philosophischen Akademie.

Stolz, K. R. 1923. *The Psychology of Prayer*. New York: Abingdon.

Stolz, K. R. 1932. *Pastoral Psychology*. New York: Abingdon.

Stolz, K. R. 1937. *Psychology of Religious Living*. New York: Abingdon.

Stolz, K. R. 1939. *Tricks Our Minds Play on Us*. New York: Abingdon.

Stolz, K. R. 1943. *The Church and Psychotherapy*. New York: Abingdon-Cokesbury.

Stratton, G. M. 1911. *Psychology of Religion*. New York: The Macmillan Co.

Stratton, G. M. 1923. *Anger: Its Religious and Moral Significance*. New York: The Macmillan Co.

Strickland, F. L. 1924. *Psychology of Religious Experience*. New York: Abingdon.

Strommen, M. P. 1963. *Profiles of Church Youth*. St. Louis: Concordia.

Strunk, O., Jr. 1970. "Humanistic Religious Psychology: A New Chapter in the Psychology of Religion." *The Journal of Pastoral Care*, 24, 90-97.

Sullivan, H. S. 1953. *The Interpersonal Theory of Psychiatry*. New York: W. W. Norton and Co.

Symonds, P. M. 1931. *Diagnosing Personality and Conduct*. New York: Appleton-Century.

143

Symonds, P. M. 1939. *Psychology of Parent-Child Relationships.* New York: Appleton-Century.
Szasz, T. S. 1960. "The Myth of Mental Illness." *American Psychologist,* 15, 113-18.

Talbert, E. L. 1933. "On Francis Galton's Contribution to the Science of Religion." *Scientific Monographs,* 15, 205-49.
Teilhard de Chardin, Pierre. 1959. *The Phenomenon of Man.* New York: Harper & Bros.
Teilhard de Chardin, Pierre. 1964. *The Future of Man.* New York: Harper & Row.
Thomas, G. F. (ed.) 1944. *The Vitality of the Christian Tradition.* New York: Harper & Bros.
Thomas, O. C. 1962. "Psychology and Theology on the Nature of Man." *Pastoral Psychology,* 13, 41-46.
Thouless, R. H. 1923. *Introduction to the Psychology of Religion.* New York: The Macmillan Co.
Tillich, P. 1946. "Religion and Health." *Review of Religion,* 10.
Tillich, P. 1952. *The Courage to Be.* New Haven: Yale University Press.
Tillich, P. 1957. *Dynamics of Faith.* New York: Harper & Bros.
Trotter, W. 1916. *Instincts of the Herd in Peace and War.* New York: The Macmillan Co.

Ungersma, A. J. 1961. *The Search for Meaning.* Philadelphia: Westminster Press.
Unwin, J. D. 1934. *Sex and Culture.* New York: Oxford University Press.

Vogt, Edward D. 1968. "Religionics: A Neglected Approach to the Study of Religion." Paper read at the 1968 meeting of the Society for the Scientific Study of Religion. Montreal, Canada, Oct. 25.
Van Kaam, A. 1962. "Religion and the Existential Will." *Insight,* 1, 2-9.
Van Kaam, A. 1968. *Religion and Personality.* Garden City, N. Y.: Doubleday & Co.

Watson, J. B. 1919. *Psychology from the Standpoint of a Behaviorist.* Philadelphia: J. B. Lippincott Co.
Watson, J. B. 1924. *Behaviorism.* New York: W. W. Norton and Co.
Weatherhead, L. D. 1935. *Psychology and Life.* Nashville: Abingdon Press.
White, R. W. 1959. "Motivation Reconsidered: The Concept of Competence." *Psychological Review,* 66, 297-333.
White, R. W. 1960. "Competence and the Psychosexual Stages of Development." In M. R. Jones (ed.), *Nebraska Symposium on Motivation.* Lincoln: University of Nebraska Press.
Whitehead, A. N. 1925. *Science and the Modern World.* New York: The Macmillan Co.
Wieman, H. N., & Wieman, R. W. 1935. *Normative Psychology of Religion.* New York: Thomas Y. Crowell Co.
Winkler, R. 1921. *Phaenomenologie und Religion.* Tübingen: Mohr.
Winter, G. 1961. *The Suburban Captivity of the Churches.* Garden City, N.Y.: Doubleday & Co.
Wise, C. A. 1942. *Religion in Illness and Health.* New York: Harper & Bros.
Wobbermin, G. 1921. *Systematische Theologie nach religionspsychologischer Methode.* II. Band: *Des Wesen der Religion.* Leipzig: Hinrichs.
Wobbermin, G. 1925. *Systematische Theologie nach rleigionspsychologischer Methode.* III. Band: *Wesen und Wahrheit des Christentums.* Leipzig: Hinrichs.
Woodburn, A. S. 1927. *The Religious Attitude.* New York: The Macmillan Co.
Woodger, J. 1956. *Physics, Psychology and Medicine.* Cambridge: Cambridge University Press.
Wright, W. K. 1922. *A Student's Philosophy of Religion.* New York: The Macmillan Co.
Wright, W. K. 1924. "On Certain Aspects of the Religious Sentiment." *Journal of Religion,* 4, 449-63.
Wunderle, G. 1922. *Einführung in die moderne Religionspsychologie.* Munich: Koesel & Pustet.
Wundt, W. 1902. *Facts of the Moral Life.* New York: The Macmillan Co.
Wundt, W. 1902a. *Principles of Physiological Psychology.* New York: The Macmillan Co.
Wundt, W. 1916. *Elements of Folk Psychology.* New York: The Macmillan Co.
Wylie, Ruth C. 1961. *The Self Concept.* Lincoln: University of Nebraska Press.

Index

Hume, D., 124
Hylan, J. P., 14, 50

Ich und das Es, Das (Freud), 56
Idea of the Holy, The (Otto), 113
Idolatry, 112
Illusion, 104, 114
Image, 101
Immortality, 38, 47
Individuation, 107
Inge, W. R., 40, 79
Inman, T., 50
Instinct(s), 33, 38, 43-44, 46, 79
Instinct and Reason (Marshall), 33
Interpersonal relationships, 90
Introduction à la vie mystique (Lejeune), 17
Introduction to the Psychology of Religion (Thouless), 48
Introductory Lectures (Freud), 56
Introspection, 26, 38
Inzest-Motiv in Sage und Dichtung, Das (Rank), 59
Ittelson, W. H., 126, 127, 129

James, W., 15, 16, 18, 19, 46, 47, 72, 73, 74, 76, 99-101, 102, 103, 109, 116, 117, 118, 123
Jastrow, Jr., 40
Jastrow, M., 48
Jeans, J. H., 55
Jesus, 46, 50, 60, 62, 84
Jesus the Christ (Hall), 46
Johnson, F. E., 128
Johnson, J. E., 118
Johnson, P. E., 75, 94, 111, 118, 132
Jones, E., 44, 52, 55, 58, 61, 79, 102, 104
Josey, C. C., 75
Jung, C. G., 58, 79, 81, 87, 88, 89, 92, 106, 107, 122, 132

Kant, I., 12, 67, 102
Kapital, Das (Marx), 42
Kautsky, K., 42
Kelley, G. A., 130
Kierkegaard, S., 80
Kilpatrick, F. L., 127
Kinast, 16
King, I., 16, 43, 74, 81
Kirkpatrick, G., 132
Koepp, W., 39
Koreshanity, 42
Krafft-Ebbing, Richard von, 110
Kuelpe, O., 26
Kueness, 40
Kunkel, F., 79, 81, 88

Lancaster, E. G., 13, 73

Langer, G., 61
Langley, G. H., 32
Lapsley, J. N., 121
Lawton, G., 45
LeBon, G., 43, 44
Lejeune, P., 17
Lenin, N., 42
Leuba, J. H., 13, 17, 18, 25, 31, 34, 36, 38, 47, 48, 73, 74, 76, 77, 101, 102, 117
Levy-Bruhl, L., 45-46
Lewin, K., 91
Libido, 50
Lidgett, J. S., 33
Liebman, J. L., 95
Ligon, E. M., 54, 84
Lindzey, G., 131
Link, H. S., 55
Love, 115, 130, 131
Lutoslawski, W., 32

McClelland, D. C., 125
McDougall, W., 33, 78
McGiffert, A. C., Jr., 94
McKenzie, J. G., 79, 93
McLaughlin, B., 124
Maimonides, M., 130
Maladies des mystiques (Charbounier), 17
Maladies du sentiment religieux, Les (Murisier), 17, 50
Mana, 44
Marbe, K., 26
Marbeck, O., 61
Marechal, K., 54
Marett, R. R., 44, 55
Marshall, H. R., 33
Martin, E. D., 36, 37
Marty, M. E., 128
Marx, K., 42, 71
Maslow, A., 127, 130, 131
Mass, 65
Massenpsychologie und Ich-Analyse (Freud), 56
Masserman, J. H., 110
Mathews, S., 21, 33
May, R., 94, 126, 133
Mazdazan, 42
Mead, G. H., 90
Meaning of Sacrifice, The (Money-Kyrle), 53
Meehl, P., 100
Meissner, W. W., 118
Meland, B. E., 50, 55
Melanesians, 44
Melanesians, The (Codrington), 44
Menninger, K. A., 89, 90, 110, 131
Mental health, 100, 105, 108, 118, 126, 127, 130, 131
Messer, A., 26